Magpie
Rising

MAGPIE RISING

SKETCHES FROM THE GREAT PLAINS

MERRILL GILFILLAN

VINTAGE BOOKS
A DIVISION OF RANDOM HOUSE, INC.
NEW YORK

FIRST VINTAGE BOOKS EDITION, APRIL 1991

Copyright © 1988 by Merrill Gilfillan

The following publisher has generously given permission
to use extended quotations from copyrighted works:
From *The Fighting Cheyennes*, by George Bird Grinnell.
Copyright © 1955 by the University of Oklahoma Press.

Library of Congress Cataloging-in-Publication Data
Gilfillan, Merrill, 1945–
    Magpie rising : sketches from the Great Plains / Merrill
Gilfillan.—1st Vintage Books ed.
      p.   cm.
    Reprint. Originally published: Boulder, Colo. : Pruett
Pub. Co., c 1988.
    ISBN 0-679-73038-9
    1. Great Plains—Description and travel—1981–
2. Great Plains—History, Local.   3. Gilfillan, Merrill,
1945–   Journeys—Great Plains. 4. Authors,
American—20th century—Journeys. I. Title.
[F595.3.G55 1991]
917.8—dc20   90-55684
                   CIP

For Martha

These sketches were written between 1983 and 1986, modest fruits of the quick-cut, the blow-through, the right rear window. After some 50,000 miles out there, there are glimpses of a loosely knotted part-time Life Work, even. What began as simple wonder and continental curiosity ends up a sort of poetic maintenance.

M.G.

MAGPIE
RISING

'm sitting on one of the high slopes of the west butte, Sweetgrass Hills, Montana, looking off over leagues of the endlessly supple and insinuating musculature of the Great Plains. It swells and rolls. It lifts and twists close beneath the skin of the earth, headier than Ocean. Of all the landscapes on the continent this one has been opening capillaries for me like no other, calls me again and again. As an arena of light and air it cries out for the elemental homage and interaction that brought me here—I'd like to unleash 50 dalmations from the coulee below and send them off fulltilt across the spaces in the sun.

At least three mountain ranges are visible (not counting the obvious backbone of the Rockies just west), small pine-clad densities hovering isolate from the surrounding plain a hundred miles and a dozen soaring buteos from here. By my figuring they would be the Bear Paws, the Little Rockies, and the Highwoods. To the south the lip of Marias River's rough cut casts a shadow. To the north Milk River arcs teasingly through southern Alberta before swinging back toward the Missouri.

Through binoculars I can make out the green and burgundy wheat elevators of scattered Canadian hamlets. There is Foremost; there is the village of Milk River. The sight of the latter rings modest ritual bells, a salient of ritual being foreknowledge of an end with the major motions mapped: In an hour I'll be driving north and pulling up before the familiar bakery there for a bag of the first and best butter tarts beyond the border.

It's middle September and the breeze has an edge. Wild rose bushes huddle russet in the draws; the low mountain maples give a matte, disenfranchised yellow. Farther off, in one of the inner folds of the orogenic system comprising the west butte, aspens are half-turned and fluttering.

One can see equally far from Lookout Mountain, I suppose, or from scores of other high spots; but not off into such an expanse of legendary untrammeled space. From the forks of the Saskatchewan to the lower Pecos in an irregular swathe maybe 500 miles wide, the wind blows and the grasses shake. As an earth feature, the plains are simply one of the most imposing regions on the globe, a zone of a million and a quarter square miles, a thing on the order of the seas or of India.

On this continent and in the psyche of its peoples the plains have always been a staggering presence, a place of myth and cliche, a place for transformation, bafflement, or heartbreak. From the east they are release from the clawing of swamp and tangle and human density. From the west they are a drop and a straightening after the kinks and strains of mountains. Entered from any direction they are new air, a joy to behold, a combination of large-scale intimidation and primordial inner acoustics.

Within the monolithic image of the plains, within the stereotypes of dull transcontinental drivers, there is constant variety and continual change. In a sensitive aerial view the various sub-regions and their perfect flora would show as diverse and intricate and colorful as if under infrared. They stand out by their individual textures and tones as surely as the distinctive components of hardwood forests in autumn. Each has its own musical theme and instrumentation like the characters in *Peter and the Wolf*. To an open eye the Staked Plains are singular, as are the Osage, the Souris, and the Querecho plains. The Smoky Hills, the Flint Hills, the Antelope, the Ree and the Red hills each have their own rhythm and stride. There are local pockets remarkable only to the keenest eye. There are scapes within scapes, but from the bold northwest plains of Montana to the Nebraska Sandhills, on into occupied Kansas and the Texas panhandle the wind blows, grasses shake, and cottonwoods in the stream bottoms rattle. . . .

There exist various and contending climatic, topographical, and botanical definitions of the Great Plains — variations on the "treeless, flat and dry" theme — each seeking to fine hone the boundaries and unravel the mystique, but for the person sitting cross-legged on the butte or driving the cattle truck across U.S. 2 or gazing from a high story in Rapid City's Alex Johnson Hotel, the essential Great Plains experience is rarefaction. Take all the vectors, passions, and psychological tendrils found, say, at a Friday night dance at a large high school in, say, the Bronx, and scatter them in an area 30 by 50 miles in extent, for example. I assume the phenomenon was very similar for the elephant hunter of western Kansas some 10,000 years back.

The effect of the spatials is more than scenic. It stirs and incites, induces movement in all its forms, rediscovers near-forgotten needs-to-be-gone. It is the horizontal charge of transversable space. The spatials of the Smoky Mountains or the Atlantic from Red Hook are meditative and inertial. The planar pull of the grasslands provokes and challenges. It is a seductive space of suction and vortex, of migration and wandering and swirl. Open to sun, open to lightning, each day and step have a distinct uncanny potential for revelation.

———————————

I'm a third of the way down the slope, heading for the car, when I realize I haven't had enough. I drove two days to do this very thing on this very spot. There's another, sharply conical hill just west of my knob, crowned with ponderosas in an inviting way. I angle across and up its flank and into the stunted grove at the top for another look south.

There are accounts of early 19th Century Blackfoot boys walking from this very region all the way to Taos to see what's there and trade or raid a little, and old-time Kiowa stories of monkey sightings that indicate penetration probably as far as the Yucatan.

It is a *dilation*, that's the word. A dilation on several levels at once, a call to inner movement as well as outer.

At the very top of the conical hill, in a small half-oven of rock I find the remains of an old fire. Someone had gathered him or her self in out of the wind, up into the rarefaction.

I poke in the ashes out of idle curiosity and turn

up a dead half-inch metallic green bee — a dazzling malachite green, a jewel of a desiccated bee and the focal point, for a mesmerized second there, of a hundred miles in all directions.

The wind blows. *Nihil obstat*. "Sheep May Safely Graze."

Two

There comes a morning every spring—a morning whose light is just so—when the first solid thought to enter the mind is *drive*. It's as predictable as lilacs and the return of the big flocks. It never fails to quash any conceivable competition: Today will be spent at the wheel, going nowhere in particular.

The map is spread across the table to be eyed over coffee. The possibilities are tantalizing as a candy store window. Highways drift across the map's pastels, soft inviting tints with something spring-like of their own. An unsung river slices through pale green; a speck of a village with a once in a lifetime name sits waiting in an expanse of tablet-paper yellow. . . .

To drive without destination, for the sake of energy and imagination coordinated and unleashed in elemental motion is as New World a pastime as baseball. The American highway system will no doubt be looked back upon one day with massive, astonished nostalgia. The age of the private motor car has evolved the Sunday drive of my grandparents into an activity as kinetically rich as, say, sailing; as evocative and honey-textured as solitary fishing.

I belong to the second generation for whom (most of whom) automobiles have been a life-long everyday experience. The Aimless Drive is well within us. A glimpse from a car window of a certain stand of trees or a random rural intersection can arouse a long gone stretch of highway past: the sudden unnameable chill of childhood vacations on the first few miles of Michigan 123 just into the Upper Peninsula, where the loom of spruce and bog and wild untameable land signals a goodbye to one sort of civilization and the highway narrows; U.S. 95 south of Needles, California, that unearthly straightaway hinting at lift-off between sundown and dark; an August Sunday morning rolling along a live oak alley between Cut Off and Houma, Louisiana, with every window open and scattered backwoods churches sending out an intermittent music. . . .

When the object of a drive is simply vernal, an April uncoiling with minimal interference and maximum sky, going nowhere in particular often means a sortie into west Kansas, where the kinetics are sweet and pure, where if there were son or daughter or Venusian beside me I would announce "You have now entered the High Plains."

As the classic representative of the true High Plains as geologically defined, west Kansas is the bulge, the remnant hump, away from which to east and west the lesser plains environment spreads. From the Texas panhandle to northwest Nebraska, through west Kansas and eastern Colorado, the High Plains boom, the undisturbed fragment of the original debris apron that is the structural base of all Great Plains topography, an apron deposited by ever-shifting rivers spilling from the ancient Rockies. Continuously worried away on both edges, the High Plains are poised there, an ancestral plateau protected by its very dryness—given any great amount of rain per year the plain's soft soils would soon be Gulf of Mexico-bound.

Meanwhile it is a perfect place to get lost at the wheel and thrive. The lonesome stretches with their frank yet infinitely subtle topographies invoke the free-form open-country pleasure of watching one's self in the imagination from half a mile above, a southbound speck in Gove County. Driving becomes a sort of gesture, an intimate interaction with the earth's surface having to do with words like *tangent* and *cosine*.

Crossing Kansas in any direction, even for the fifteenth time, is oceanic enough an undertaking to rouse the adrenalin. There are good crossings and bad, wild and dull ones. Crossings with weather and without. Green crossings, dun crossings; dicksissel or chickory crossings. There is U.S. 36, a great one, and 50, an overworked one, and 83 and 27 and 96 and little Kansas 4 squeaking through, and 160, the Oklahoma-flavored passage. They take you through villages with chunks of the late 1940s suspended intact, stowed for safekeeping: ghost hotels, ranks of green and white elfin tourist cottages gone to seed, and tiny ex-chili parlors and pool halls abandoned on weed-choked corners.

In May banks of blooming peonies toss on lawns and graveyards. If you hit it right lilacs will be aflower in 50 yard hedges on two sides of farmhouses; they perfume the air as camelias scent Louisiana. Stands of feral yellow iris shadow former homesites; if you stopped and poked around in the fencerow weeds there you would likely find an abandoned aspara-gus patch. An August crossing can be a test. The south wind will be blowing hot. Corn and small town trees lean north under its breath; the south side car window will have to stay up. In winter you will see every earthly shade of brown and every known nuance of shadow.

Driving west on 36 you will hear the last cardinal in, probably, Phillipsburg. Driving north or south you can cross in half a day some of the most distinguished of plains rivers: the Platte, the Republican, the Saline, the Solomon, and the Smoky Hill. Any eastward crossing is a descending transit moving steadily into a thickening of the air. It is the slow, 10 feet per mile drop that pulls all the folkloric freight cars turned loose on the High Plains into Kansas City. Herefords change to holsteins; black kingbirds replace gray. About Marysville you might as well be in Missouri. Up around Redwing on Kansas 4 the change will jell dramatically. To the east will open a vista of densely wooded bottomlands amid bold rolling prairie; massive thunderheads crowd the sky tier upon tier. It is a new air moist enough to furnish a new richness and a languorous haze. It is Quivira for Coronadans, the eastern edge of the High Plains overlooking something low, lusher, dewey and dreamy as an old postcard shot. . . .

Over the years the crossings meld and form a distillation from the accumulated time-exposure pleasing to high-sailing birds. In a tavern far from Kansas someone will mention Sharon Springs or Atwood or Leoti and there is instantly gathered in my mind an abstracted Kansas highway decorated with a dozen dead calico cats, a quintessential rural wedding convoy roaring by in the middle of nowhere, and an oncoming cherry red Porsche driven by what looks like a manic runaway priest, suddenly there on Highway 4 among the pickups.

——————— ▬▬ ———————

West Kansas, its irrigated civilization of the moment, is a cultural Olduvai. Scattered liberally among its normal population are unexpected and newsworthy treasures of human behavior that sometimes call for a complete reassessment of everything assumed about the species up to that point. For human types it is as rich as New York's upper Broadway.

In a small town restaurant we lunched near a man in a black net shirt that revealed a full upper-torso tattoo job featuring a portrait of Jesus Christ on the back amid clouds of navy blue roses and a stylized brunette bombshell on each upper arm. When he stood at the counter to pay his bill his chest and belly showed an admirably detailed condensation of the famous Otto Becker barroom print of Custer's Last Stand.

In another cafe one Sunday noon in a farm town there was a giant two booths down, a bona fide northwest Kansas giant with a voice like a very slow record and hands that dwarfed his coffee cup and lay across the back of the booth like big friendly beefsteaks. He was of indeterminate age; his silver-haired wife and another couple, all on the diminutive side, gazed up at him, nodding and smiling, as the Sunday small talk thundered on.

In a remote bar in west Kansas I spent 20 minutes chatting with the owner over a beer while, ten feet away in a highchair behind the bar, her two-year-old shouted at 15 second intervals, cage-bird-like, "Shit!" "Goddamn!" "You gotta piss?" over and over, smiling self-absorbedly and playing with a table spoon as the corroded little sparkplugs in his brain fired.

But of all of human Kansas the highest High Plains beauty is to be found in those modest prairie stars, the hamlets. "Hamlet": diminutive of *ham* (MF), village; akin to OE *hām*, home.

Hamlets are utterly distinct entities. Detached and austere, they occupy an ecological niche between the town and the isolate self-sufficient ranch-farm complex housing two or more generations. Hamlets have negligible commerce and none of the awkward communal success or desperate self-esteem of larger farm towns, yet they are socially more varied than the extended family ranch clusters within their windbreaks.

Hamlets are gratifyingly in-scale and honest. They represent a pure and elemental High Plains culture, as in Petri dish. Hamlets have few visible means of support; no schools; no class plays; no historical museums; little public enterprise save the occasional gas station/grocery combination.

Hamlets are by necessity occupied, but only by deduction; it is rare to see a human in a west Kansas hamlet. Hamlets hold from 10 to 100 people. They have dirt and/or mud streets; wind-bent trees; a high proportion of boarded-up homes and buildings; a good sprinkling of abandoned cars and rusty flat-bed trucks in backyards and edge-of-hamlet fields. There is usually a lovely aqua or purple late 1940s house trailer or two to be found. There are always big wooden cable spools laying around somewhere in the community and generally an overgrown quonset hut and a hypothetical hermit's tarpaper shack in high weeds.

Hamlets are silent and deafeningly humble. They exist away from major highways. The best of them have creeks or even rivers. Hamlets fade and dry up and revive like their sporadic streams; it doesn't matter, they live on the faint border of ghost town to begin with. Someone moves away. Forty years later they come back. "Hullo, Carl."

To stand for a moment in a good far-flung hamlet is to catch High Plains life through a low-toned but well cut prism. You sense the rhythm of the meagerest social stirrings, a simple huddling beneath the formidable thumb of High Plains odds. It is the gritty traction and vulnerability of the prairie dog town.

Anywhere in the west it is a solid way to move, from hamlet to hamlet. It keeps one's sense of awe toned and restores one's faith in the rock-bottom human talent to watch the very same lilac send out its blossoms for a lifetime. There is Boyero, Colorado, one of the great ones, Boyero of the free-ranging goat herd and the '59 Chevy with its windows smashed out. There is nearby Arroya with its black dog and intricate anonymous tower-sculpture of old tools and machine parts. There is Brandon, down in the Sand Creek country, with its remnant stucco motel; a faded "Showers" still glimmers from one worn wall. There is Horace, Kansas, in Greeley County, and Rolla with its piles of fenceposts. Modoc and Moscow with toilet paper in their trees. There is Sumatra, Montana, and Lothair with the guy-wired trailer post office; Russell and Bantry, North Dakota; Castle Rock, South Dakota, on its stark rise; Many Berries, Alberta, Spotted Horse and Jay Em, Wyoming; Mt. Dora (of the windmills), New Mexico; and Dickens, Nebraska, sweet with locust blow and vireos.

If I were to take a student of ekistics to just one hamlet, it would be Speed, Kansas, a mile off the state highway in Phillips County. It is large for a hamlet, with some 300 souls, but in spirit and feel it is archetypal. It is a hamlet that Turgenev might have stumbled across on one of his 1840s hunting rambles and, with a sweep of his hat, requested kvass, bread and cucumbers, and a bed for the night in the haymow. The streets are rutted mud. Hogs and horses rummage here and there. The only sign of commercial activity is a bombed out shell of gas station on a corner. Huge old cottonwoods gangle and groan above the small houses; their oriole nests sway in the wind. In a rare sighting, a woman edges across her backyard with a bucket of chicken feed and apple cores.

Somehow Speed has found its pocket, a web of space and cartilege that antedates the cooked and bobs steadily in the raw. Or maybe its collective attention has simply shifted, adapted to realms and needs that interstate travelers hardly know. Speed has settled into the plains the way some towns settle into the mountains, asking for nothing, solid in its refusal that is anathema to chamber of commerce civic pride and publicity stunt men who haunt the churchey towns.

Speed and the other good hamlets are irreducible.

Long may they huddle in the sunset. In a Speed backyard among an anachronistic array of exotic chickens,
a flock of pea fowl wades stately in the mud and
preens from rooves of junked cars, Asian and baffling.
An invisible, deduced neighbor might well have a damp
cellar full of prime orchids or an upstairs converted
for albino flying squirrels. . . . The plains provide.

And then one day we were running southwest
from Dodge City after a very bad morning in west
Kansas, a morning starting in Scott City and soon lost
in the depressing agribusiness haze and swamp, in the
humiliating funk of that rampant out-of-proportion
agriculture and its miles of chemical-soaked fields and
giant rococo machinery, its outrageous absentee-land-
lord devastation of the Arkansas River bottom east
from Pierceville, wheat jammed in to the very banks,
leaving not a single tree for 20 miles along one of the
continent's major rivers. It is a fouled mess and
monotone, an ignoble extreme of the slash and burn.
So we cut back southwest from Dodge looking
for a patch of sage or a burst of yucca, watching for
the first upright thing after that valley market-muck.
We were running from some riffless abstraction wide
as weather, and knew enough not to pass through
Liberal that day, Liberal where street directions are
consistently given in relation to fast food joints.
We were getting hungry but refused to consider
any restaurants, the spleen was running so high—no
cloned $4.95 buffet this time. We wanted to break

the seal and flag the inertia. Leaving Sublette we shared
a clipped fantasia peopled with small-time itinerant
curry stands along the west Kansas roads; wandering
po-boy vendors, their carts tinkling in the speckled
shade of Chinese elms; now and then a big gypsy fish
fry making good use of its continent at a forsaken intersection. Or at least beef, there's plenty of that around
Dodge. And honey, we saw a lonely flock of hives
way out there along some little creek, a token of some
sanity. Beef and honey; beef stewed in honey-water
with a sprig of sage, sold by the snowcone cup. . . .

Shit, as the kid in the bar would say. We
snatched a handful of lilacs from a semi-public bush
in Satanta (named for a Kiowa chief) and took a
lesser highway northwest toward Ulysses (Grant
County). We stopped out there somewhere and picked
enough young dandelion greens for a salad, threw in
some leftover radishes and dressed it all up with two-
day old chili vinaigrette from the cooler. We ate it
with crackers, sitting in the thick grass and buffalo
gourds between the railroad tracks and the road.

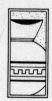

THREE

Some topographies are so arranged that the human niche is obvious at first sight; transplant any sensible population to the area and they will soon drift to and mark their effective place in the landscape.

The Loup River country of east-central Nebraska is ample, borderline *saftig*, compared to much of the Great Plains. Lying between the 98th and 99th meridians it partakes of a lushness that is essentially midwestern. The Loup curls wide and easy, its various headwaters having risen in the Sandhills and converged some 40 miles west of here. Its bottom is densely wooded, the flat valleys fertile. Half a mile from the river the bluffs rise, modest largely treeless hills of even stride where white farmhouses sit tucked above the flood plain, overlooking the tillage. That is where the humans live, for the most part; where they have always lived. That is their level, their watermark in this valley and others like it.

Dreamy enough farm country, but nothing of crackle in that alone. You must wait for sundown for the Loup's specialty, its particular and unique phantasm. The way one drives to the Texas hill country for the bluebonnets or finagles a night in Kansas City for the barbecue, I stop here east of Genoa for the night to take in the Pawnee stars.

From about 1680 to 1730 the Skidi band of Pawnees perched their earth lodges on these Loup River hills and tilled the bottomlands below. The Skidi and the other Pawnee divisions were unique among North American natives in that they came from the sky: They traced their ancestors back to a celestial parentage involving the pursuit and eventual persuasion of the Evening Star by the Morning Star. This was something new for the continent. The Arikaras came from the earth in the form of corn; the Arapahoes sprang from the legendary floodwaters; the good people of Dannebrog, Nebraska, came from Eden via Denmark and New York. The Pawnees came from the stars.

To Pawnees watching from the domed rooves of their earth homes sidereal movement reenacted the pursuit myth again and again. The entire nightly westward movement of the heavenly bodies represented a sexual drama related to the very creation and renewal of human life. All of Pawnee life was imbued with sky, as much so as the Mayans. The astral imprint is understandably deep on any people living a good part of their lives outside, in relatively open country in a relatively harsh world—the exposure of a population to the full night sky over centuries; those big wheels turning in the common eye; dependable stars in a deciduous universe.

So the Pawnees planted their crops by star calendar and priests charted the seasons and kept the people informed of the comings and goings of the sky heroes. But the suffusion went much deeper than such practical concerns, it burned as deep as identity and vocabulary. Each Skidi village was descended from a particular star patron; this star, back in the creation days, provided its village with a sacred bundle and accompanying ceremonies, the village taking its name from its star bundle.

As creation magma cooled and the political sense

and need jelled, the early Skidi settlements gathered to form a political union, a loose blood federation of star-strung villages. Looking at one another, thinking of one another off there up or down the river, but linked by the sky-set, the Pawnee priests did the natural thing: The five core groups of the federation each positioned their new village in relation to the other sites on the astral model, each stationed and built according to its star of origin. Thus we had on earth for a few generations a human constellation, the *Skidi constellation*, the stars mirrored on Loup River.

"It is fair to say that the Pawnees were obsessed with the sky," writes Von Del Chamberlain. They sensed that the universe is charged; the source of electric life was the flicker of the evening star. Even their early earth lodge structure had a celestial base: dome of sky, four corner posts representing the four earth-quarter stars, the smoke hole of certain priest houses serving as equinoctial sighting guides. One of the important star bundles held an oval buckskin chart of the heavens accurate enough that many of the bodies have been identified by modern students — evidence of a sophisticated and long-working astronomy. As part of the infamous Morning Star sacrifice — a female captive despatched in a ritual dictated by celestial conjunctions — the party of warriors en route to enemy territory to capture the intended victim slept around the fire in strictly prescribed configuration according to the celestial affiliation of the mythical character each man portrayed. . . .

And so walking out along the dusty road to see

the Pawnee stars come out means finding an entirely
new set of figments in the sky. Instead of Cassiopeia we
have *parus* the rabbit. The two Ursas form a pair of
constellations known to the Pawnee as the "stretchers":
men carrying a wounded ally as a healer walks beside.
Sagittarius is now a bear, Auriga a mountain lion.
There are ducks and loons and wolves and a circle of
chiefs. And with a leap of scale and association
nearing the quantum point, the sky as a whole registered in the Pawnee head as a speckled bobcat pelt.

It is a curious and potent option to walk beneath
a different, reconstrued night sky. The evening is
humid, almost summer-thick. Early insects drone from
the river brush. Craning up for so long my brow
and back trickle perspiration. All this meshing of the
astral and the inner, this gaping wide-eyed in the
dimensionless darkness, reminds me of John Lilly in
his sensory deprivation tanks, floating in 93 degree
water alone with the interior night sky and the hum
of two constants: the blood moving in the veins and
the purr of the nervous system.

Now the mosquitos show up. Sky and culture.
Retina and culture. Suffusion via the priesthood. To
sleep in constellation array around a small fire. . . .
To walk around through mud and bugs *as stars*. . . .
Aiee—it's too hot to think about all that. Astonishing
that it stood right here, it all has the feel of a vanished
cathedral, but it is still comforting to visualize a
sizeable segment of Pawnees whose chief pleasures on
earth were corn and marrow stew and cold water
on August days.

The Encyclopedia Britannica describes constellations as "fossil remains of a primitive mythology." The Pawnees left the Loup in the mid 1870s—the combination of Sioux and white trash was too much—for the Oklahoma Indian Territory, taking a few bags of wild plum pits with them. Today there is a monument or two, a village site preserved along the Republican River, and their faint wind-blown stars that still come on each night, secret forms flickering amid the standardized Mesopotamian versions.

Next morning as I drove east down the river that place's emblem and echo, a flag for that Loup country, was there in the scattered starry herds of white Charolais cattle and their brand new snowy calves grazing against the green Loup valley hills.

Four

ach morning in the various towns we get up early as possible for a walk through the half-asleep streets and alleys. The earlier the better to catch the quiet backside before the citizens are afoot and the small gears turning. This morning, a cool May one, it is Fort Sumner, New Mexico. Fort Sumner *sur* Pecos, and we circle out slowly, paralleling the main street, taking in the rested roses hushed on trellises and the piles of cast-off tires—cool to the touch, fragrant even in the stillness—piled slapdash behind an automotive store. Empty backyards, old basketball hoops with torn and rotting nets, new half-spaded gardens, tricycles and toys in a vacant lawn at 6 A.M.: suspended and completely lucid between the dreamy and the Pompeian.

We stop eventually for breakfast in a main street cafe; we are the first customers of the day. The owner-cook-waitress talks of Denver as she works the griddle, mentions a few intersections to substantiate her indistinct stories. The sourdough biscuits hot from the oven were made from sourdough starter begun 45 years ago by a local ranch wife. But the ham was bad, too old, and we sneaked it into a napkin to dispose of outside and spare the old woman's feelings.

We walk out to the edge of town toward the river. The day warms and a light haze hangs over the irrigated hay fields in the bottomlands, their fragrance still heavy from night. Passing back down the main street we peek in the windows of the sprawling Billy the Kid museum, an old-time tourist attraction full of guns and pictures and regional oddities like "petrified dinosaur droppings."

Billy died a few miles outside of town in 1881, shot in pitch of night at a friend's house. He came to the area now and then to see a girlfriend. Today the Fort Sumner Eagles Club calls itself the Billy the Kid Aerie and a surprising number of tourists stop at the Kid's grave. He is buried in the old fort graveyard, next to a modern baseball diamond within sight of the Pecos. Old Fort Sumner is famous as well as the holding pen for the wild Navajos rounded up by Kit Carson in 1863 and brought to nearby Bosque Redondo. It was here that Navajos, suddenly sedentary, turned their energies to large-scale commercial weaving.

Billy's tombstone reads "The Boy Bandit King— He Died as He Had Lived." Across the top are 21 notches framed by the caption, "21 . . . Men." Like James Dean's, Billy's headstone has been coveted and stolen by playful necrophiles more than once. It was lifted in 1950 and not recovered until 1976 over in Granbury, Texas. It was taken again in February 1981 and found again several months later in Huntington Beach, California (probably not all that far from the heisted James Dean stone). Today the Kid's marker rests beside a pair of his buddies in the grip of anchored iron shackles behind a stout cage fence.

The Pecos is good company out here, rich and aromatic. Scissortailed flycatchers and their young consult on the telephone wires, the offspring clumsy with half-length tail feathers. The Pecos is a border announcing the southwest edge of the Great Plains. Upstream a hundred miles or so she cuts through the

New Mexican mountains in her early stages, through
an old Hispanic culture of valley villages since 1600,
through juniper nook-and-cranny country long domesti-
cated. The little villages up there have a composure,
an unhurried poise even in architecture that recalls the
concentration of the remote Appalachians.

As the river leaves the mountains south of Las
Vegas, the old Hispanic culture follows for a ways,
extending out to adobe hamlets like Colonias and
Puerto de Luna. Near the well-named latter, Coronado,
tolled by the metal gold, built a log bridge over the
Pecos, what turned out to be a metaphorical bridge
from one culture area to another unknown and blistering one. Coronado's army would learn the deadly
side of the plains, plodding along with their sheep and
cattle, constantly thirsty and usually lost, driven by
sky and mirage to leave piles of buffalo chips as
markers for their own rear guard and to build huge
fires and sound trumpets each night to guide in the
wayward hunters and scouts, and that bridge come
to appear as dubious entry to a savage ocean, a door
with no floor on the other side.

Following the Pecos down from Santa Rosa the
border clarifies. Behind, across the river to the north
and west stretch nearly solid junipers. To the east,
open grasslands with here and there an adventurous
evergreen or a cholla and the red dirt showing through.
Looming beyond on the eastern horizon the dark
high mass of the Llano Estacado. Nearing Fort Sumner
the evergreens slough entirely, give way to yucca- and
sage-dotted grassland. We are out in the open again.

Downstream from Billy's grave the Pecos moves through runty brush plains, scrubby red dirt–mesquite country. The Llano is always there to the east, bruise-colored, threatening like a motionless storm on the skyline. If we threw in a small pterodactyl dropping in a bottle at this point, in several days it would find itself in bulling water near the mouth, surging stolidly through a stark canyon across the formidable scrub of south Texas to hit the Rio Grande just above Del Rio. And from the right tree or rooftop in Del Rio you might be able to catch a glimpse of the Balcones, the rocky outcropping marking the southern-most extent of the Great Plains; I don't know. Mostly, facing north, there is a gradual but distinctly promising rise from the Rio Grande valley. Either way, Del Rio and the mouth of the Pecos will serve as south point for anyone circumnavigating the plains.

Political borders like the Rio Grande harden and reinforce themselves over the years, but biologically the river here does mark an edge of sorts, a rather narrow transition zone between tropical and temperate fauna. There is a stretch of San Felipe Creek on the east side of Del Rio notorious in the right circles as the upstream limit for the diminutive green kingfisher, a Texas specialty. That gets us out early, after a chorizo omelet, and sure enough there it is, buzzing along the creek and fishing from the retainer wall.

Out of town toward Mexico we take a dirt road paralleling the border and park to work the brushy tangle for an olive sparrow, another specialty of the

region that soon accommodates by leaping to the top
of a small tree and breaking into song. We walk
down the dusty road toward the Rio Grande. Ditches
are strewn with old socks and kitchen garbage, a car
seat and a checkered sport coat. Painted buntings —
those birds you never get used to — sing from the wires.

From the road's end you can see the Mexican
village of Acuna in pastel patches through the trees.
Acuna was for some time a major peyote exporter to
the tribes of Oklahoma; reputedly a good share of its
economy derived from the gathering and dispersal of
the buttons, in a classical example of tropic feeding
temperate, of suction from the north, the way the Indies
seasoned Europe and Italian woodwinds sweetened
18th century France, traceable as a jet stream. For a
century the old curanderos and border hustlers have
sent their medicine to the shell-shocked, penned-in
southern plains people. Smuggled on cattle drives or
driven as far as Montana by the suitcase full, it is the
hot ancient sending its dark-side discoveries north.

There is a campground a few miles north of Del
Rio where I would like to spend a week with a good-
sized charcoal grill and a supply of local Del Rio wines
in homage to the south point and its flow of hot
chiles and bushels of purple garlic and its paisano food.
The supermarkets of Del Rio, the meat departments
in particular, offer a range of cuts deserving at least a
week to sample. It would be an immersion. With a bag
of little red bird chiles the size of sunflower seeds we
will sit there eating and glancing north now and then.

There will be roast kid; lamb head (slow barbe-
qued, the slivers of meat then plucked from the bone
and mixed with green chile sauce); *tripas* and pork
tails, beef feet and lamb tongue stew.

The grand finale will have to be the *machitos*, a
package at the H.E.B. store at $1.79/pound: goat
liver and goat heart wrapped in beef leaf-tallow and
bound with goat gut. The whole bundle goes over
low coals for hours. We'll set it up to catch a nice south
wind, put some big roasting heads of garlic around
the edges and let the aromas waft north over the plains
as is their wont.

FIVE

THE DEATH OF MOUSE'S ROAD

remember reading as a child, curled on a sofa, stories of the plains tribes by the hour. There was the narrative excitement, of course, but what lingered, I see now, what took root and ripened, were the place names, the rivers, ridges, and ranges, the *geographic word* softly detonating and filling the head till my inner ear roared as of conch shell.

Thus a geography not one's own forms in the mind, firms on a lattice of pregnant place names. It is a private mythic geography that interlocks with one's past through the most intimate means, the language.

On the plains, "where place names are widely scattered," the toponym is heavily loaded to begin with by virtue of its high relief. But to come up against the actuality behind one of those names throwing echoes to a book devoured in 1957 in the wooded midwest is a lustrous event. The magical names beckon and when you find them in their places, simply and solidly there as always, they are familiar as a childhood object.

It is the closing of a long-open loop to set foot, 30 years later, on the Judith Mountains or the bone-dry Arikaree River or dozens of other spots of ground with names worn smooth by years of quiet subconscious surf. It is tribute to the place and to the original young head that incubated and held the words. It is pilgrimage most fruitfully made only after that unmistakable time when one's childhood sets as a distant and topographically distinct world, continually receding from that point on, a rumor-misted far-flung province to be handled, governed, bartered with, visited on high occasions, entertained. . . .

The plains have their good share of blood stains. A casual glance from a car almost anywhere on the interstates is bound to take in the scene of some anonymous strife from aboriginal days or the 19th Century wars. Butte, creek, arroyo: setting for surprise, chase, slash for life.

The soil of Europe with its long heavily populated history and massive-manpower wars seems saturated with a sort of dense past. In time the vastness of the plains will no doubt accumulate its own, but today there is still a gentle tension in the imagination between the outright vacancy of the land and its points of intense human voltage; between erasure, the absorption of event by space, and its erstwhile adrenalin and anchor, *right here* or *right there*.

The brief story of the death of Mouse's Road, a Cheyenne, as recorded by George Bird Grinnell, is one of those heightened choreographies of human action classical in its lines, of the cut of Rilke's *Lay of the Love and Death of Cornet Christopher Rilke*. It bestows a burnish on the generality "headwaters of the Washita" and deserves more than the half-day we drove that country, down around Mobeetie and Old Mobeetie and Allison, and over toward the Oklahoma line, crisscrossing and watching the hills, flirting with the place, wondering about that unknown, lost-forever point in space.

Mouse's Road and three friends were surrounded on a hill after stealing horses from a Comanche/Kiowa camp. Shortly, Mouse's Road was the only Cheyenne left alive.

Early in the fight Mouse's Road's bow was broken in two by a ball, and he threw it away. A Comanche chief, seeing him thus disarmed, charged up to kill him with his lance, but Mouse's Road avoided the blow, caught hold of the Comanche, pulled him from his horse, and killed him with his knife. Mouse's Road was still unwounded. He let the Comanche's horse go, and signed to the Kiowas: "Come on."

There was a man named Lone Wolf, a chief and a brave man, who had been behind the other Kiowas. He called out: "I have just come and wish you all to look at me. I intend to kill that man." He said to a Mexican captive: "Do you ride close behind me." The two charged upon Mouse's Road, and the Mexican rode straight at him, but Mouse's Road, though on foot, did not run away; he ran to meet the Mexican and, springing at him seized him, pulled him from his horse and plunged his knife into him several times. While he was doing this Lone Wolf dismounted and rushed up to help the Mexican. Mouse's Road dropped the dead Mexican and rushed at Lone Wolf, who ran at him with his lance held in both hands above his head. . . . As he thrust with the lance Mouse's Road stooped and ran under it, caught Lone Wolf by the left shoulder and struck him a terrible blow with his knife in the hip. Lone Wolf turned to run and Mouse's Road caught him by his hair ornament and with all his force thrust at his back. The knife struck one of the hair ornaments and broke in two, leaving about four inches of blade on the handle. Lone Wolf screamed for help to his people, but no one came, and Mouse's Road continued to stab and hack and cut him with the stump of the knife until Lone Wolf fell to the ground, pretending to be dead.

Now came a Comanche chief riding a fine horse and armed with a lance and bow and arrows. Mouse's Road took up the lance Lone Wolf had dropped and ran to meet the Comanche. He parried the Comanche's lance thrust and drove his own lance into the Comanche and lifted him high out of the saddle, and the Comanche died.

Now the Comanches and Kiowas saw something that they had never seen before—a man who seemed swifter than a horse, more active than a panther, as strong as a bear, and one against whom weapons seemed useless. There were more than a hundred of the Kiowas and Comanches and only one Cheyenne on foot, without arms, but the Kiowas and Comanches began to run away. Others, braver, made signs to Mouse's Road, who had now mounted the Comanche's horse: "Hold on! Wait, wait. Take that horse that you have. We will give you a saddle. Go on home to your village and tell your people what has happened."

"No," signed Mouse's Road, "I will not go home; my brothers have all been killed and if I were to go home I should be crying all the time—mourning for these men. You must kill me."

When he said this, all the Kiowas started to run, and Mouse's Road charged them. Behind the main body of the enemy were two Kiowas who were just coming up. Both had guns, and when they saw Mouse's Road coming they got off their horses and sat down and waited until he was close to them and then

both fired. One of the balls broke his thigh and he
fell from his horse. Yet still he sat up to defend
himself with his lance and the Kiowas and Comanches
dared not go near him. One crept up from behind
and shot him in the back and he fell over. Then all
the Kiowas and Comanches rushed on him and cut
off his head, and when they had done that, Mouse's
Road raised himself and sat upright.

The Kiowas and Comanches jumped on their
horses in fright and fled to their village and told the
people they had killed a medicine man and he had
come to life again and was coming to attack them.
And, the women swiftly packing up a few of their
things, the whole camp moved away, leaving many of
their lodges standing.

The Kiowas and Comanches said that Mouse's
Road was the bravest man they ever saw or heard of.

All this one day in the 1830s on maybe that sagebrush
rise, or that one with the three white gas tanks
visible from Route 83.

The theatre of the plains' space cries out for
human gesture of fitting magnitude, ample of dimension
yet humble under a full sky. The plains tribes knew
it, did it right, by necessity but by prescription as
well — stringing the line of human love and war and
grief out long and tungsten thin.

As in the common and spacious convention of
the early plains, "Going after the bones." As in 1870,
in the spring of that year, the Kiowa Set-angia's son
was killed while raiding in Texas. That autumn, Set-

angia, heartbroken but discreet enough to allow the
scavengers time, traveled south, retracing his son's trail
in high mourning, river to river, following the meticu-
lous oral directions, found the site and the beloved
bones, wrapped them in fine blankets and brought
them home on a red horse. He carried them with him
the rest of his life. Two years earlier Stumbling Bear
had led a party of Kiowas across the Llano Estacado
to the upper Canadian to find and bury the bones of
seven friends killed the preceding summer by Utes.
There are numerous examples of similar month-long
missions; in them all the space, the grievous ride,
were major aspects of the business: patient corteges
worthy of their landscape.

That brief-blooming world of the mounted plains
tribes (a phenomenon of three or four generations) is
a world so foreign, so lavish in some ways, and so
utterly, so recently gone, that it tends to lift and float
into a realm resembling opera: a universe set aside
and raised slightly, rendered loud, flamboyant, and
hair-raisingly gorgeous. It is endlessly, maybe instinc-
tively, tempting to set that entire human phase in
amber, in perpetual full regalia, sweeping across a vast
cosmos of passion and pageantry as self-contained
and remote as "Arcadia" was to 16th Century Italian
operateers; as imaginary, bubble-enclosed, and sunlit
as the "Italy" of Shakespeare.

And so we made a short station for Mouse's Road
and his airborne friends with a taste of George Dickel
on a knoll in the blood-soaked, forgetful upper
Washita country.

Six

Driving north from Nunn on Colorado 85 you reach a point where the plains rear and assert themselves, lift toward piedmont, almost crackle. For the plains lover, for those who have made the modest quantum leap beyond loving mountains, this is a stretch to sit back and whistle under the breath. Then, just as you settle into a steppe frame of mind, you crest a ridge and there is Cheyenne, Wyoming.

The mild surprise has a lot to do with "Why here?" There's no river to speak of; Crow Creek, a small tributary of the South Platte, is handy but hardly charismatic. Cheyenne was platted by geo-political near-chance. The Union Pacific tracks being laid west from Omaha in 1867 were due to pass that way and southeast Wyoming territory needed a supply center. The settlement passed through the predictable boom-town hellhole stage, then grew entrenched outfitting gold-seekers bound for the Black Hills and taking Texas beef off the hands of trail-weary herd bosses.

Old Fort Russell's red brick Virginian layout was updated to become Warren Air Force Base in the 1930s and in 1957 was chosen to house-sit with the nation's first Atlas ICBM. By now it is control center for some 200 missiles in the Wyoming, Colorado, and Nebraska network. You might run across Cheyenne Air Force boys out in the Nebraska panhandle greasing or tidying up one of the many missile silos that carbuncle the Great Plains. One bright morning in Weld County, Colorado, we met an entire crew under gun-ship and armored car guard cautiously moving a missile on a long-bed Air Force blue truck from one pit to another.

The "magic city of the plains," now numbering about 47,000 citizens, still has a thin-rooted roofless quality that matches its peculiar and nearly perpetual High Plains breeze, a breeze flirtatious and chipping, full of deja vu and something like ocean, especially when it raises its voice to a scream. It's at its best on the edge of town, which seems to be nearly everywhere in Cheyenne. Except for a few corners in the five-block-square downtown proper, the plains are usually present, peeking between shopping centers or nonchalantly rippling away behind a junkyard.

Cheyenne sits 6000 feet above sea level. Her space has a bargain feel and even city time is reasonable—parking meters ask 25 cents for two hours. If you have occasion to take a cab twice in a Cheyenne day, odds are good you'll get the same driver. There are always a few folks on the streets who look like they've just blown in from the hinter, a bit down at heel and slightly overwhelmed. There is a kind of bus station feel, and sometimes a touch of the dotty. But Cheyenne, like most open places, has always had a strong sense of itself and its context, its geographic fate: A major hotel that burned in the '20s was named, with breathtaking understatement, the InterOcean.

Tonight the chilly wind is tossing the piped-in street corner Christmas muzak around. The streets are deserted and a snowy lilt of plain shows to the southwest. It's a good night to look around Cheyenne again. To loiter around the western store windows, catching up on the latest Tony Lama exotics and the pointed rubber overshoes cut to fit them. And to keep up with recent innovations on the jackalope theme in a corner souvenir shop. I see one full-body mount and two head mounts featuring real rabbits and real antlers in addition to several synthetic Disneyesque versions probably commissioned in some mystified Asian sweatshop.

Looking down one of the main north-south streets you can see the Wyoming capitol hunkering at the end in a rather strained way, but the obvious heart of Cheyenne is the lovely old Union Pacific station and its bordering circuitry of tracks and towers, its steady revving of yard engines, its jolts and clanks in the night. Cheyenne is still a railroad town, though its role as major dispatching center has diminished in the last five years. The yards are busy for this day and age and you see plenty of railroad men shuffling through town at odd hours, hurrying for a train or just off one, tired, with satchels and empty lunch buckets.

Some cities hide their freight yards, segregate them as wild fenced-off places. In Cheyenne they border the main street front and center. The old hotels clustered downtown within a few blocks of the depot tell the story. The Stevens, the Plains, the Albany, the Rex, the Wyoming, the Top, the Pioneer. Many of them are defunct; small three-story turn-of-the-century bricks amoulder with little left but their worn signs or a weak pentimento blurb on an alley wall. But there are still murky Melvillean places where you can take a room for 11 or 12 dollars and while away an hour with the railroad boys in the threadbare half-flight-up lobby. A dusty elk head shines in TV light; an old saddle hangs on the upper bannister. . . .

Heading east on Lincoln Way, cutting by the Lincoln Theatre (both names stem from U.S. 30, the Astoria-Atlantic City "Lincoln Highway"; between Cheyenne and Laramie on Interstate 80, route 30's successor, a huge bust of Lincoln looms oddly at Cheyenne Pass), I swing by a refurbished corner house to see a minor point of interest, the "Phillip Whynott, Attorney" sign, and then cut north to the old Frontier Hotel on 19th at Central for a glimpse, by penlight, of the plaster bas-relief fresco by its door: a cowboy portrait from the '20s or so, a head and shoulders shot of a pure and high-minded man in a stetson with a wonderful *tabula rasa* look on his face.

There is bad news on 17th Street: The Mayflower Cafe has gone under, or elsewhere, or fishing. . . . In any case its prime rib is no more. The Mayflower was a classic of cafe eclecticism, with a yawning home-style dining room where lackluster redecoration could not hide a fingerprint old as the hills. Its walls held large namesake Massachusetts seascapes that resembled 16th Century European visions of a New World the artist knew only through rumor. The two-mimeo-page menu offered 20 lunch items, not counting sand-wiches, and a dozen "special dinners" ranging from three lamb chops with pilaf to baked Long Island duckling with apple preserves ($6) to the prime rib that reminded you how beef got its reputation. The calf's liver was "Holstein" and the spaghetti was "Italian."

This sort of restaurant is not necessarily rare.
Every year or so you will run across one in Gallup or
Bismarck or eastern Iowa; not to mention San
Francisco's famous Sincere Cafe, featuring a bargain
Belgian hare in a dizzying menu that handles like a
Homeric catalog. When you read "Old Fashioned
Chicken-Fried Steak" beside "Mountain Trout Maitre
d'Hotel" you know you're there.

The challenge is always finding, by luck or
hearsay, the one or two edible items on the board. At
the Mayflower the faces were always memorable and
the local conversation was solid as landscape; yet much
of the food was terrible. (One late lunch there the
boiled beef tongue and spinach were sodden enough
I had to knuckle down and concentrate on the way the
interior of the place reflected the spatial effects of the
city outside and on how the five waitresses at station
30 yards across the room might well be High Plains
sisters judging from their skin tones.) But there are
other things. . . .

———————————

For decades the Plains Hotel was home for most
railroad men laying over in Cheyenne. Since the Union
Pacific bought a motel of its own just up the street
things are quieter in the five stories of the Plains. An
old timer dozes in the lobby and the banquet and
conference rooms on the mezzanine are borderline
ratty, entropic. On the stairs I pass a few teenagers
who seem to know where they're going.

Room 440 is blessed with a Union Pacific view

across 16th Street to the tracks, the station with its huge badge aglow, the new control tower, the blinking lights of the Albany bar sign. To the south, refinery lights and snowy plains vague in the darkness, looking Russian and harsh. A cold man with a hot thermos crosses the parking lot below, making for a train.

In the old days Cheyenne was a bona fide transportation center, not only as a turn-around point for some 30 trains a day but the early base for several western airlines as well, and, given the Lincoln Highway, a motorcar and trucking oasis of high profile.

The railroading was the last to go, or weaken, when computerized dispatching and trainmaking shifted the nerve-center to Omaha. The old roundhouse was demolished soon after; there is an aerial view postcard of Cheyenne still on the market that shows it well. Contemporary big-unit freights carrying homogenous loads of west coast containers or coal rarely need to add or drop a single car on a run halfway across the continent. Crews have been reduced accordingly and a future of 100% radio-controlled freight trains is not inconceivable.

It was, I think, the second time I passed through Cheyenne—we were headed north, didn't even get off the interstate—that I heard by chance a broadcast of the Union Pacific callboard on local radio: a fast-moving, jargon-laced report given three times a day, announcing rotation schedules for enginemen and trainmen, eastbound and west. Who's up, what train, and what she'll be carrying where. Names and numbers and cities. Sometimes there were more personal

touches, messages for families, or quick lists of in-
coming crews so roasts could be popped into ovens.
UP wives went about their daily business with
transistor radios at their sides. Much of the report
was impossible to decipher but the gist was clear
enough to make the spine tingle: the species on the
primal move in a primal setting.

After 22 years KRAE dropped the callboard in
October 1985, two months ago as I write in the Plains
Hotel. Trainmen now call a toll-free number for a
blasé recorded message out of Omaha. I had hoped
to listen to it up here in 440 watching the American
and UP flags snap and flap in unison across the way
and the big floodlit Greyhound sign crack and peel.
The callboard always reminded me of the fragrant
shipping news column I read casually in the *New York
Times*, the way I glanced at coast-to-coast college
football scores—arrivals, departures, shadowy destina-
tions—and would have been perfect company on this
cold inter-ocean night.

SEVEN

"It was a time of day
and year I knew well."
— *Proust*

There is a brief Fall passage, usually in September, like this morning along the Little White River in South Dakota, when the light/temperature combination precisely matches that of early Spring and the willing birds are half inspired to crank up a ghostly rendition of their breeding music. There is a kind of eerie displacement in hearing a robin caroling this descending time of year. Half a dozen flickers are chasing about in the river bottom, giving their *wicka-wicka* calls and displaying their bright undertails as they do in mating season. Chickadees whistle their spring songs in the ponderosas and redwings in their marshy spots beside the road are in full song when the first sun strikes.

In towns the house finches will be warbling above kids walking to school and starlings will be chuckling and *whew*ing from the maples as the thermal units, as phenologists call those distilled measures of light/ heat, hit the same frequency on receding (the angle of reflection) as they do on arrival in March (the angle of incidence). These days we catch the slightly run-down mirror image, a far traveled biological echo.

Overhead a steady drawn-out spool of blackbirds drifts south and will continue all day. Chokecherry bushes are crowded with migrant birds gleaning leftover fruit. In a small dead pine on the hillside there rests for a moment one of those peculiarly autumnal mixed flocks of unlikely blend—a female grosbeak, a tanager, chipping and white-crowned sparrows, three flickers, a small flycatcher, a pair of Audubon's warblers, all within an eight foot reach. Even a hummer touches down for a second. One of those motley preoccupied flocks that the old-time bird painters loved to conjure, with their feel for the horn of plenty. They seem contrived sometimes in the books but they have their actual referents in September and October. There are good ones in the densely populated Theodore Jasper plates for Studer's *Popular Ornithology* (1881), a suite of naive lithos featuring, for example, half a dozen conveniently gregarious warbler species on a single snag with a tiny church steeple rising above a village in the far background.

Phenology (*phen*omena plus *logy*) represents the human eye, the human grid, within the long-playing figure 8 of the sun's seasons. It is the observation and application of relationships within repetition, relationships between the advance of the season and the timing of its particulars. In its purest forms phenology has always been found in the simple correlated memoranda of rural people: "Plant corn when oak leaves are the size of a squirrel's ear."

Phenology is also a gambit against omnivorous abstract time, a human placement within the cyclical, within the drone of the hammered-home. Phenological time is a flexible external time, luxuriant and practical, with no sharp edges. It moves through a matrix of full-bodied particulars infinitely more viscous than calendar time. It is rendered in the eyes and ears and body rather than fermenting in the mind.

The co-incidences on which phenological time rests invite, demand, the inclusion of space. As the Pawnees ranged the upper Smoky Hill country on their annual summer hunt, someone, the women no doubt, watched the progress of the milkweed pods. When the pods reached a certain stage of maturity the Pawnees knew it was time to return to their villages on Loup River, 400 or 500 miles northeast, to tend to their corn fields. This is lush, concrete time in a perfect plains setting: kneeling in the wind, checking the milkweed time; doing one thing in reference to a *distant other*.

Yesterday morning I drove early into the town of Mission. There was a hint of frost-shock on the roadside grasses; coots were muddling in occasional small ponds. At the main intersection downtown I noticed an old Sioux gentleman bundled up in a long woolen overcoat, bedroom slippers, and a baseball cap edging along the sidewalk with his cane, working his way through a throng of halfbreed sidewalk dogs until he reached a sunny spot. There he stopped, lit a cigarette and squared back against a brick wall to soak up the welcome 8 o'clock rays.

I thought of a familiar heart-of-winter detail from my midwestern hometown: the delicate helio-choreography of the village pigeon flock as they gathered on cold January mornings on the courthouse bell tower roof and, as one, shifted with imper-ceptible little sidesteps around its various facets throughout the day to catch the maximal warmth.

And I remembered an out-of-luck family at a road-side park in west Texas one May. They were operating out of an old pickup truck with a makeshift canvas roof on the back. It had rained and hailed hard for three straight days, but now it was over. That noon they were all stretching, hanging damp clothes and musty blankets from branches and bushes and carefully spreading soggy Pall Malls on a picnic table to dry in the sun.

I passed the old Sioux man, the old man and the sun, half an hour later. He had moved to the now sunny northwest corner of the intersection and was sitting, beaming and smoking, on a low wall. By 10:30 when I drove through town again after running errands he was over on the east side by a boarded-up building, resting in the shade.

EIGHT

The gumbo plain of north-central and eastern North Dakota is a throw point for much of the continent's water. The plain is a slump of thick, poorly drained glacial debris that turns rivers like a straight-arm. To the south and southeast the flow runs to the Gulf of Mexico via the Missouri and the Mississippi. Waters to the north sog and creep to Hudson Bay.

The Souris River, the stream I have been dallying with for several days, rises in southern Saskatchewan and drops casually south into the U.S. until it hits the gumbo plain; at that point it reverses itself and curls back into Canada and joins the Assiniboine River near Brandon, Manitoba, having delineated a tongue-shaped chunk of North Dakota that by its willows and fens is as north-country as Labatts.

The wheat country up here is mercifully broken by stands of flax, sunflowers, and mustard. The grain culture has captured the North Dakota political mind so thoroughly that some of the state's official actions smack of widespread ergot ingestion. With a surplus of wheat large enough to depress prices and necessitate North Dakota's 85% partaking of federal funds to *not* plant, the wheat farmers continue to drain the ecological gems of the region, the thousands of potholes that render the state the major wild duck producer in the nation. Some 20,000 acres a year, ditched and converted to wheat tilth. It takes a nasty and sometimes child-level struggle to save even minimal wetlands in North Dakota with the pro-drainage and generally peeved state government consistently blocking any federal, or even private, efforts to acquire and preserve pothole areas.

On the other hand, North Dakota ships 20 million pounds of its mustard seed to Europe. Much of the German brown mustard and the Dijons on our tables has come, via the great trade routes, from the northern plains.

There are jokes about North Dakota. In general they resemble jokes about Newfoundland or Poland or the Minnesota lutefiske stories to the east, but the brunt is usually the landscape. Stuff like, how lucky Custer's men had been—at least they didn't have to march back across North Dakota. The state retaliates (a verb appropriate to much of its policy) with billboards at its borders such as "You are now entering Minnesota. Why?"

An acquaintance had recommended a cafe in tiny, out-of-the-way Heimdahl with good homecooking at 1950 prices, where the locals sat around drinking coffee and eulogizing the great "amber waves of grain" era and remarking on how everyone seemed to be moving away from town. After a few days in North Dakota I had been in four cafes where all the ingredients were identical, pretty much interchangeable. Wonderful misshapen home-cut donuts rolled in sugar and set out on an old china plate on the counter; eggs fried in real butter; German meat pastries called fleisch keukla that cry out for local mustard, though the local populace stubbornly eats them with ketchup; lots of coffee; and endless bitching. Lost, pathetic, hinterland bitching with the long-shadowed sadness of the called third strike. I decided not to digress to see Heimdahl.

High in North Dakota, near the border, the Souris River is simply the Souris—French for mouse. But farther south, near the point where it wheels and heads back to Canada (a Canadian wag could make a joke about that in itself), the bridge signs suddenly proclaim it to be "Mouse River." Although no one could explain just why, I got the uneasy impression that the North Dakota legislature had gotten testy again, mad at Canada for, probably, crossing one of its drain-the-prairie plans and didn't want any "Canadian" words on their river signs. The Boeotian.

In the middle of this white man's burden and kettle of ripe fish there is a stretch of the Souris in Bottineau County that is like a fine narrow carpet laid on an asphalt parking lot. It is the preserved prairie stretch of the J. Clark Salyer National Wildlife Refuge, a five mile section along the river where native grasses still flourish and sway.

The Souris and its lush life is a pleasure to behold, but today the upland, the mixed-grass prairie, is magnetic. Maybe I have never seen it just right before, in just the right August mix, in full growth and color. I walked out earlier in the hot sun for a quick look. The grassland's proportions and intricacies are wondrous as trees are to children by their very looming and cut of leaf. Then, among the trees, we pressed their various leaves and climbed them and learned them in winter by their postures and their miens. Now it is the same for me with the grasses. To walk out among those *tribes*, as botanists call them, broaches a new array and enters a new scale to fathom and run.

The grassland beauty is a supple and flexible one of soft tones and absorbency. Needlegrass, bluestem, switch and wheat grass—each has its own range on the late summer pastel spectrum. Russets and beiges and straws in delicate navel-high mix for miles—for five miles anyway—along the Souris, brightened by splashes of goldenrod and gayfeather, all nodding and tossing in the wind, all catching the sun like hair on an arm.

Down along the river the cordgrass grows, the slough grass, tall and tough, a bottomland species so thick in the 19th Century that prairie settlers cut it and stored it for fuel, twisting the hay into bunches, doubling and knotting them into manageable clumps that would burn for ten minutes; a day's supply could be cut in an hour.

On higher ground, big bluestem, the "turkey foot" bluestem, is just blooming. This is, at first glance, a modest occasion. But on close inspection it is a miniature botanical event of Keatsian richness. The tiny male and female parts dangle furry and luxuriant from the nodding heads, light green and yellow, with a delectable, succulent look and texture, an ampleness as of cashews hanging from a cashew bush.

Farther on a detached stand of Indian grass is abloom as well, even more striking, with lavender-magenta male parts poised above the pollen-yellow female, each a sixteenth of an inch long. There is even a very faint honey-like aroma. The poise of the minimal as seen from afar shifts to the close-up beauty of the working parts.

There is little bluestem, taking on its familiar red-bronze, the indelible shade that will color otherwise drab winter prairies. There is sideoats grama, the streamlined handsome grass called "banner-waving-in-wind grass" by the Sioux. There is needlegrass, whose tightly wound awns can twist their way dangerously into sheep mouth or dog eye. And many I can't find in my field guide.

There is the Prairie Sandreed, the showy grass whose broad plume Crazy Horse wore in his hair instead of a feather. . . .

The sun finally drops to a bearable angle. For two hours I have been resting in the narrow lee-side shadow of the pickup, half dozing or watching assorted ducks on the Souris and a flock of white pelicans playing peek-a-boo with me from the far shallows. Willets and yellowlegs are gleaning along the vehicle-wide mowed access road nearby, looking strangely chicken-like as they scratch and peck a hundred yards from water.

Somewhere out there on the North Dakota plains the little grasshopper mice are stirring, readying for their nocturnal hunts: little known carnivorous rodents voracious as shrews. They not only stalk and attack their invertebrate prey like larger predators; they even howl like miniature wolves.

Somewhere out here on the Souris prairie within sight of the truck scurries a sparrow I have looked for in vain for two consecutive summers and have just driven 900 miles to seek again. Somewhere out there

Baird's sparrow lurks in the grassroots shade, an archetypal mixed-prairie creature dependent enough on
that certain thin blend of habitat that its population
has fallen drastically in direct relation to the turning of
the native prairie grasses. A legendary will-of-the-
wisp and the last bird painted by Audubon, Baird's
sparrow draws scores of birders to its North Dakota
breeding grounds each season.

During the past two summers I have walked many
miles through what I took to be perfect Baird's
habitat. Through central and southern Alberta, into
Saskatchewan, around and around Lake Pakowki
south of Medicine Hat. South through eastern Montana, straining the ears at dozens of points along
secondary roads, listening for the legendary giveaway
song, that "bell-like tinkle" in the "breathless, tinkly
timbre" that I imagined more than one night as I
drifted off to sleep near Saskatoon.

So, somewhere out there this afternoon there are
Baird's sparrows, the bird so prairie-oriented it often
builds its nest in the hoofprints of cattle. By 5:00 I
can't wait any longer. I take a quart of water and a
Granny Smith and strike off through the prairie tribes,
off through the billions. I keep the sun on my left or
quarter away from it. At each step a handful of grass-
hoppers bursts from the cover (the grille of the truck
has a half-inch coating of high protein grasshopper
pemmican-paste). Monarch butterflies drift and eddy
southward. Far to the east the Turtle Mountains
hold shadows.

It is all poised and lovely, but the birds are tricky

as always in the grasslands. I flush dozens of
sparrows from the grass in an hour of slow walking;
they jump and fly off low and twisting or rise high
and simply drift away out of sight or drop a quarter
of a mile away into other faceless cover. Some are
recognizable: the tail of the vesper sparrow, the call of
longspurs. But the good view is rare. It begins to
feel desperately like those mornings around Lake
Pakowki, Alberta.

There is solace in a bright sharp-tailed sparrow I
nudge into close view wading through a dried up
cattail patch, but the foreboding is there. I break the
frequency and walk over to the fence separating the
preserve from an endless wheat field. Piled here and
there are massive rock stacks 50 yards long and 8
feet high, cleaned up glacial debris resembling the huge
bull-dozed stump piles left in the midwestern soybean
country, similar agricultural aftermath.

Right there, at 6:45, turned away along the
fence, I hear it off behind me. It registers instantly as
Baird's song and sends a flurry of chill up the spine.
It is a lovely, minor key little song, wistful and care-
free at once, delicate as crystal, simple as breath.
More than that, or part of that, it is a new song to
these ears; it is a new configuration, as in snowflake,
of the given world.

I take a drink and head back toward the song.
There are several singing now, scattered across the
prairie. As I walk closer the songs seem to shift, to
sing away from me. I see sparrows flash and drop in
the distance; when I advance a hundred yards in that

direction, the songs are suddenly behind me or off to my right. There is a distinct feeling of coyness.

I choose a near-at-hand song, a good sweet one, and move towards it very slowly on hands and knees. Every ten yards I raise up and scan any possible perches—a spot of buckbrush, a prominent stand of bluestem (one of the field guides portrays Baird's sparrow swaying on a turkey-foot bluestem)—hoping to pick out the singer by chance. And there it is, pretty far off, but it's Baird's beyond a doubt, on a low green clump of something or other.

I pick a convenient stand of tall grass six feet across, roughly between myself and the bird. Using it as cover I make a quick crouching charge some 50 yards towards the spot. From behind the clump I catch my breath and slowly raise the binoculars over the top. It's still there, I'm in good range now, and at long last I see him eye to eye, and then the ochre head thrown back in song.

I watch him till he flies, then lie back in the grass for a few minutes just listening to the three or four Baird's songs drifting in from the surrounding acres. Walking back the two miles to the truck I meet families of black terns leisurely quartering above the prairie feeding on insects. And I see another Baird's, a good view in late light; but it is always the first one we remember.

Back at the truck I make coffee and get out the George Dickel for a toast. Coots and geese cackle and squawk down along the Souris. From the lawn chair I watch the big Dakota light fade and the big single headlight of a combine working a field down the road to the east.

For half an hour there I am completely satisfied with the world, my life, and everyone else's. That fragile two-toned song is still in my head with that evening prairie light that stirred it, golden through the grasses, the hair on the arm. It is a new song for today and for life. It is something to whistle for Olivier Messiaen, the gentle Frenchman with the fine ears who finds and transcribes a huge semi-sweet and musical God in the songs of birds.

Back to business. Throw a willet feather in a vial into the Souris and it will end up in the Hudson Bay via the Assiniboine, the Red, the Nelson.

NINE

CHEZ DALTON

The flag down in here shows a scissor-tailed fly-catcher above a road-killed box turtle. It flies above the Coffeyville, Kansas, square this hot silent Sunday noon. We stand in the shade of the Southern Sun Tan Center. The bricks in the street read "Coffeyville V. B. & T. Co." We peek in the Dalton Museum and the old bank. Up Death Valley, four open-eyed mannikins (donated by J.C. Penney?) lie stiffly commemorating the dead gang. Graffito on the lintel above: "Get stoned with the Daltons." Down the street a lone man sacks stray cans around a quarry.

———————

Combines work the Monday fields around Meade. A pair of Mississippi kites hangs over the edge of town. The Dalton hideout house on the south side has six American flags and one mulberry tree in front. We peek down the secret escape tunnel from house to barn. The house was owned by the Dalton sister. "Then she moved back down to Kingfisher, Oklahoma."

At the Meade Sonic Drive-In I eat a foot-long coney, ponder the "pickle-o's" on the menu (dill pickle slices dipped in chicken-fried steak batter and deep fried), wipe the chili sauce from my sunglasses, and go on.

22–23 June 1986

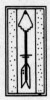

TEN

n the primal juniper-piñon country south of Pueblo, Colorado, there runs a perfectly human-sized arroyo, six feet deep and shoulder-wide, snaking through the rabbit-brush and cholla, a minor secret way through those long, tilted, evergreen-studded plains. This is the upper Arkansas zone of giant cinnamon rolls and magnificent geological poise. It is mountain-related country, a cusp of things southwestern, Rocky Mountain, and planar. The land has the feel of the rugged becalmed and balanced in some ancient asymmetrical way; of mayhem outlasted. There is something chilling about the piñons and their landscape. They hint of wandering pedestrians, of seed eaters, of Cabeza de Vaca, and perpetual hunger. In this context, sooner or later I remember that arroyo, the arroyo just in its prime and perfect human fit. I recall it as a latent luxury on some scale, as a pure conduit and place of shelter from something voracious like giant birds of prey.

Traveling east and a little south, one leaves the handcut sandstone architecture of the juniper country — entire ranch spreads built of stone from the buttes and outcroppings above — and enters the dust-bowl architecture of southeast Colorado, the weary brown stucco farmhouses amid corn and milo stubble in fields of pitiful soil. Some of them are no more than hulks, remnants from the infamous '30s, their windmills long-gone and fallen, with a lingering tree or two around the rotting tank.

Descending into Kansas, I find smoke from scat-

tered ranches announcing the April rite of burning
tumbleweeds that have drifted high against fences and
sheds all winter. Then, of a sudden, there is the
Cimarron below. Viewed from the Point of Rocks, a
modest landmark in any other setting but an invaluable
one on the Santa Fe trail, the Cimarron meanders
away to the northeast. Rising on the plains (only the
Saskatchewan, the Missouri, the Platte, the Arkansas,
and the Canadian rise in the mountains and completely
cross the Great Plains), the Cimarron is dry much of
the year, an undependable watercourse with a ferocious
name. Its flow is intermittent enough to allow stands
of tall grasses to creep in on higher elevations of the
bed itself. Skunk, deer, jeep, and six-inch wild turkey
tracks cross and follow the sandy channel. The valley
on both sides is savannah-like with its blond grasses
thriving among gangly cottonwoods.

In 1941 the river actually flooded, ferociously,
and rose even to the base of this outcropping. Among
other effects, the floodwaters exposed a graffiti auto-
graph of Francisco Coronado carved in the stone,
dated 1541. The carving (apparently authenticated at
some level or other) was stolen by vandals before it
could be protected and preserved, but Coronado
consciousness sprang to life in southwest Kansas. There
is a village named after the man himself and one
named after Montezuma (a tenuous extension) featuring Mexican street names. In Liberal, a short walk
from the "Dorothy House" as transplanted from "The
Wizard of Oz," there is a Coronado museum with an
imposing statue of Francisco with sword.

I pack plenty of water and fruit and start downriver from my Cimarron camp, following the bed
along the reddish stands of salt cedar, but soon cut
south, up into the high sage and yucca, and follow
the river from the distance of a mile or more. Up here
the short grasses are just showing a hint of green new
growth and the knee-high sand sage holds tiny new
leafage. A single cane cholla is the tallest plant around.
Cassin's sparrows sing invisibly in the brush.

Looking for scaled quail, a south of the Cimarron specialty, I head for a distant windmill, the sort
of landmark gathering place favored by coveys. A
faint sound I question as some sage plains creature
turns out to be a flock of snow geese going over
nearly out of sight. At the first windmill, on second
glance, I spot half a dozen quail loafing in the spindly
shade of the tower. When they see me they run like
miniature ostriches across the clearing and into the
grass. So reluctant are these birds to fly that early
settlers patiently herded coveys into wide V-shaped
fence-wings leading to netted cage-traps, exactly as
plains tribes drove herds of ruminants over cliff
kill-sites.

On a high ridge with a faint lip of sandy blow-
out four miles downriver I sit for a drink and an
apple and look at the Cimarron away and below, the
great cottonwoods just beginning to color and lighten
in the upper branches as the big sticky buds French-
simmer and twitch in the year's first 80 degree days.
They are the only visible trees in the landscape, not
counting a far ranch on the north side uplands with

its dark-trunked windbreak and grove, no doubt more cottonwoods with a mix of Chinese elms.

Where there is human life on the plains there are cottonwoods. Where there is any hope at all, there are cottonwoods on the horizon. Large abstinent trees with an unpretentious dignity and a delicious merciful shade, they are fuel and shelter; a place to hide; tea (from the inner bark) to cure gastric upheavals from *gyppy* (alkaline) plains water; emergency tipi poles, wickiup frames, hobo hut struts; yellow dye from early spring buds at the juicy stage they're in down there today; pirogues, if you like, on the order of the big upper Missouri versions of the 1860s, from cottonwoods four to six feet thick hollowed and lashed together double outrigger style, with a capacity of ten tons.

An often overlooked cause of Indian outrage at white immigrants on the plains—long before the buffalo were seriously threatened—was the wholesale destruction of the cottonwoods of the Smoky Hill and Republican River "Big Timber" areas, long-time and crucial wintering grounds for various tribes, where the mainstay fodder for the sizeable horse herds was cottonwood bark.

The big trees have a raw-boned beauty all their own—they anchor some of Bierstadt's flightier landscapes—but first and foremost, shade, and often water, and stabilizing familiar groves for eastern tree-people, a cool psychological harbor.

Up here in the treeless I think of poor John Clare, the copse-loving English poet driven to madness by, in part, the enclosure laws of the early 19th Century, the change in the agricultural mind and process that disrupted and delocalized ancient patterns and cycles through the fencing and geometrization of the land. And John Clare, the vulnerable man, was so attached to his particular Helpston locale—"the place he knew and everything he knew," as John Barrell puts it— that to see an individual tree he had known daily for 30 years felled—*gone*—was painful, more than painful, as it crashed in his internalized landscape.

Flux and vegetation. Trees and the mutable. There is a different sense of permanence out here in the grasslands where the only lasting points of reference are dirt and stone, where one rarely takes a bearing in the deciduous. It is hard to love a particular yucca, say, the way John Clare did an oak, in an entangling alliance sort of way. . . . That may be part of the prairie balm.

I move on another two or three miles, warming and falling into the rhythm and deep happiness of anonymous walking at its highest level, the Great Plains pedestrian. It is curiously reminiscent of nights of absolute freedom on upper Broadway, New York, those long pointless and exhilarating walks from 96th Street to Times Square and back. I drop back to the Cimarron to pick up the thread that brought me here, the idea of a descent, a river descent at its most subtle extreme, a descent without water, but there all the same. I wanted a long day *that* slow, that low-water slow. Unglamorous (you will not likely meet Edward Abbey on these plains rivers), hot and thirsty, but an act of reclamation on the cranky old infamous Cimarron, reclaimed in the name of the wandering useless and the simple cool drink in some archetypal August. To let the Cimarron know it's not forgotten.

I return to camp just before sundown, hot and thirsty indeed. As I put together a fire the faint croakings of a sandhill crane flock comes into focus and I watch them go over, north-bound, the leader casting a knowing eye at the river certainly etched on the cranes' ancestral route charts, if nothing more than as a dry river *manqué* to be passed up most years. I wonder where he'll put them down for the night.

I wrap half a dozen new potatoes in foil, stick them along one side of a good cottonwood twig fire, and set a can of beans on the other. I see a west-bound jet pass over at the same time each evening, for Los Angeles maybe, like a regular friend. The first Great Horned Owl hoots across the river as the last light on the big curve of the Cimarron illumines the hummocks of bunchgrass, turning them golden-russet against the sand. The small patches of new growth are mint-hued in soft light.

On the inside of the bend stands one of those patriarchal groves of trees that have been there a good while, majestic and worthy of John Clare. On the outside of the bend, the shore that takes the brunt of the river in water-time, there are no trees at all; sand sage grows down to the very lip of the bed. There's the distant *putt-putt-putt* of a gas well downstream. I go back to smash and salt and pepper those potatoes.

They are sweet as roasting ears. The Cimarron has her trees exactly where she wants them.

It is yet full dark when I climb into a Forest Service blind on the edge of a Lesser Prairie Chicken lek two miles south of my river camp. I open the narrow viewing slot and settle in to wait for the birds. The first hesitant sounds of the awakening plains drift in from the dark. The bawl of a calf far-off. The first tenuous tinkling of a horned lark. Five seconds later, all in good time, a cock pheasant crows; then a burst of coyotes, a single plaintive killdeer cry. The day stirs and gathers.

Then, coming almost as a surprise in its eeriness, its disembodied quality, the first prairie chicken: a high gobble-like gulping, sometimes described as a yodel. Immediately other males join in to form a throbbing chorus, pulmonary and urgent. Small hairs rise on my arms.

As first light seeps in my field glasses pick up vague forms as the birds strut and circle about the lek, a yucca-free, short-grass zone some 50 yards in diameter. The males inflate their red air sacs, raise their horn-like neck feathers, and square off, leaping into the air, then suddenly deflating and squatting two by two, facing each other a foot apart, like cats.

The light is nearing full now. Around the edges of the lek latecomers, probably females, stand on the *qui vive*, their slender heads and necks visible above the vegetation. The low-angle sunlight illuminates the old grama grass heads. A male horned lark lights on a yucca stalk 15 feet from the blind, catching the new warmth, his tiny horns, too, bristling, his yellow throat deep as any yellow in the world, the yellow of dandelion. He is as lovely as any warbler.

On the horizon I can see the village of Wilburton hull-down three miles south and the grain elevator at Rolla to the east. But the attention invariably snaps back to the chickens—that weirdly orchestrated and organized gathering. Something rooted in the grasslands and sage, yet social, floating just above the earth as well. An electrical current in the zany meat-life zone. A parallel, a reminder, and even a model. Dance and strut and feather bustle. The Lakota word for *flute* (an important courtship instrument) means, literally, "great (as in powerful) prairie chicken."

I sat there for an hour, letting the pores open, the music register, and the trees fall and rot where they may. I was basking in a High Plains constant, a sound as elemental as dripping water. Harried and hemmed in, the prairie chickens go about their brilliant business. Even the herefords that wandered by at one point—free-minded herefords who see a great many High Plains secrets in a day—stopped at the far edge of the lek, chewing and watching in mild bewilderment for a moment before plodding on.

ELEVEN

CHRISTMAS 287

The main street of Clarendon, Texas, is full of cotton
blow as the surrounding countryside is full of cotton wagons. The stray fluff accumulates at the curbs
and gathers at the steps of public buildings and in
business doorways and freshens greasy gas station lots.
It skitters across the highway like snow, taking over
in a quiet way like cottonwood blow takes over
midwestern towns for a week in summer, drifting
thick on car windshields, covering washes hung on
the lines and coating farm ponds, low-key but dominant, like the aroma of cognac in Cognac.

Clarendon's main street is truck-rocked U.S. 287,
the Port Arthur to Choteau, Montana route. On this
particular section during this Christmas week, one of
four cars carries skis on the roof and is headed for
Colorado—this is the great Texas ski route, Herodotus,
the ski route through the cotton.

East from Clarendon we drive deeper into the
Osage Plains. We ride and watch the painstakingly slow
drop to the east; we drop east into the south, off
there, where the cotton came from. At the gins along
the road pressed off-white rectangular bales the size
of small school busses stand. The odd mechanical
cottonpickers rest here and there in the fields. Cotton
blow sticks on the roadside weeds and dapples
the berm.

We cross Red River at Estelline. In small villages
the dark silhouettes of bare pecan trees still holding
their split empty husks become more frequent, grow to
motif status. Near Vernon, in some of the huge cotton fields of what are known as neo-plantations, the

bolls still hang on the spindly leafless cotton plants. It is suddenly a radical double-take landscape: the crisp white bolls speckling against the deep red earth of the fields against a lacquer blue sky with a blowsy fluff of three-quarter moon.

We cross Pease River and drive into Vernon (birthplace of Jack Teagarden) for a bite at the Herring Cafe, on Pease Street, and make a modest contribution to the tupperware box on the counter marked "Donations for Homemade Jelly." This morning it's grape, very nice, a winey red color with buckshee flecks of butter in it. From here all the way on down 287 the spare winter trees are full of mistletoe.

Twelve

Dakota Notes

"Italian music in Dakota."
—*Walt Whitman*

Giovanni Battista Fontana, Vivaldi, Frescobaldi, Bach, and Handel fit the geography, the lay and the hang, never dissolve or wander: the watertight form of the music, its presence as a sound, shrewd configuration that does not bolt or stray in wide places.

———————

A few weeks touring the backside with one of those amphibious railroad crew pickups convertible at the crank of a crank from highway to train track use and the pocket atlas with railways marked in red. . . .

———————

White River, S.D.: "They used to close the gate up at the Big White River bridge at 9:00—no one got in or out."

They have the corner of Roosevelt and Rodeo streets. Their outfield fence is built of lilac hedge.

———————

Eagle Nest Butte: *Vision* (vision-seeking as one of the distinctive aboriginal plains culture traits) and *visibility*. Civilizations measured for one sort of inner capacity by their *intimate use of high places*. Song/dream/private consultation . . . and then, the communication creature turned completely inside out like a sock, the TV relay towers rising atop the buttes.

———————

Roe says the striking preponderance of pintos on the aboriginal North American plains (there were virtually no paint horses in aboriginal South America during the same period, 1600–1800, regardless that both continents' herds sprang from the *same parent stock*, the conquistadors' horses raised and readied on Caribbean islands) might be explained by the North American natives' deep-seated reverence for white creatures, hence an eagerness for white breeding stock that encouraged the sporting of those light genes. Or by the meshing of a straightforward delight in spotted ponies with a mysterious process of extraneous pre-natal influence—there are early examples in old testament pastoral accounts—set in motion on these plains by the literal painting of solid-color horses in one's herd to keep the desirable pinto image regularly before the wide and rolling eyes of conceiving mares.

———

An endless desire for more. And everywhere the countless roadside sunflowers, looking.

THIRTEEN

was wending through the north edge of the Black Hills in early August. The creek banks along Spearfish Canyon road were so bright with forget-me-nots I stopped twice to wade through the eye-blue stands.

Somewhere southwest of Cheyenne Crossing I finally registered the steadily increasing density of motorcycles on Highway 85, a strung-out swarm negotiating the winding road. Bikes of all kinds, from luxury Gold Wings to big haywire hawgs. Among the classic denims there were occasional college boys and a sprinkling of plump middle-aged couples with bulging saddle bags and matching weather gear.

Now I remembered following a pair of serious bikers in full regalia for a long stretch north of Torrington, Wyoming, that morning. They rode side by side with easy but marked purpose, leaning forward slightly and cupping their sunglasses each time they hit the wake of an on-coming semi; easing close together now and again for a shouted word.

Approaching Deadwood I knew I was in the middle of something major. The road was running at capacity. There were small camps of tents, lean-tos, and custom vans with a fleet of resting Harleys at every pulloff for miles out of town. Groups of big bearded men in t-shirts and vests lounged with their black-clad women below canyon box elders. Shadowy solitaries sipped beers along the stream. There must have been 500 cycles parked in a large municipal lot in downtown Deadwood. Bikers sauntered through the assortment looking it over like horseflesh or shopped for provisions in nearby stores. Between Deadwood and

Sturgis itinerant t-shirt, belt buckle, and black lace panty stands were operating from flat-bed trucks and step vans. Hand-stencilled signs tacked on the ponderosas every mile offered Harley parts and repairs. Something major. Bikers have been congregating late summers in Sturgis since 1940 for a week of bike talk, party, riding and racing, and who knows what. Last year some 45,000 showed up.

I tend to prefer the Black Hills from a good distance, from which they live up to their name, hovering pine-dark and pine-scented on the skyline, and show themselves to advantage for what they are, geologically: one of the three main eruptions in the High Plains, along with the Raton mesa outcrop and the Pine Ridge escarpment just south of the Hills. Near at hand they have in my experience been overcrowded and abused by the worst of the tourist world, large family bands looking for Mt. Rushmore, and the entire region honeycombed with diverse religious camps and retreats.

But that day, the Hills full of bikers and their molls, felt good. It was as if the Black Hills had been wand-touched and changed, utterly repopulated overnight, the culture glaze cracked and split open on a populace who lived and worked for one relatively noble reason: to ride the curve of the earth on as many days a year as possible.

I loitered in Sturgis a while, hooked by the sheer surprise of it all, the dust, the costumes, the stark bouquet of the mentality. Sturgis school kids lined the streets agog watching the particulars roar by.

Then I continued up Highway 79. I had planned
to camp at Bear Butte, a long-time holy place outside
Sturgis, but every campground was full of choppers,
so I headed north for the Slim Buttes country a couple
of hours away. That stretch of road is one to make
the heart stammer in some foreign tongue—a left-alone
short-grass country, spacious pastoral land with a
sprinkling of sage and delicate buttes on the horizons.
George Catlin, somewhere in his writings, no doubt
from some elevated point overlooking a scape like
this one that swells like choirs and organs, proffered
the notion of making the entire Great Plains a national
reserve, or whatever they called such things in the
1830s; to keep it, let it be for the peoples and wildlife,
he thought, leave it as untrammeled space, a spiritual
reservoir different from mountain wilderness. Something for the free-flow, for the nonsedentary and the
footloose eddies. There is still a segment of this continent's population who would prefer free gasoline to
free food on the conviction or instinct that endless
driving is perhaps the last physical free-zone and posi-
tive act of unlanded refusal.

I thought of this for 80 miles on that breathtaking
road, then pulled off into the wooded uplift of the
Slim Buttes, drove into the pines a couple of hundred
yards to spend the night. I built a small charcoal fire
in my collapsible K-Mart grill, just enough to heat up
leftover chicken and roast two ears of Colorado corn.

After a few minutes I hear a Harley engine down
at the highway; the short quick revs means it's thinking. Then it *vrooms* a bit and hedges in little jerks

up the side road toward me for a ways, never coming into view. It's a couple, Sturgis-bound of course, pulling off for a sandwich and rest before the last leg. I hear them laughing and goosing down below me for 20 minutes. Then they remount, ease her back down to the highway, and zoom south.

Shortly after daylight I drove the 10 or 12 miles into Reva. There was no cafe, nothing but a store– post office hybrid connected to a home, but the woman tending shop would make coffee if I wanted to wait.

She was fire worried, out there in Reva surrounded by grasslands late in a very dry summer. She had heard three fire calls on the scanner the night before, "all of them about 10 o'clock, just before the rain started. We were lucky last night; all summer it's been dry storms, lightning and no rain. It strikes the hay stacks."

She made other small talk of a sleepy sort but it was obvious her mind had been on storms and their range fires for a long time now. "I'm surprised there weren't any fires in the buttes last night the way it was lightning. Well, maybe there were and they won't find out till today."

I sweetened my coffee to go, bought a box of fig newtons and looked at the rack of tough leather ranch gloves. As I said goodbye and started for the door she said with a watery, helpless kind of smile, "Well, I wonder if there's another one building up for tonight."

From Reva I cut west and north to pick up the

Little Missouri River at Camp Crook, South Dakota, and follow it down into North Dakota. This is sagebrush country, mile after mile of open fenceless range and sage flats, the eastern edge of the Wyoming look. The road is a good one, gravel, and hangs within sight of the river most of the way to Marmath. Pronghorns are common, browsing through the sage in small herds, a lone buck here and there. They are exceedingly mysterious for so large a mammal. Built and honed for great spaces, they vanish and reappear at will, waver like mirages. There is something primordial, pre-mammalian about the pronghorn, seeing them kneeling in the sage, minimal and ascetic, their protruding eyes as big as those of a horse, registering nearly a 360 degree vision. They are drawn to some of the oddest of human artifacts on the plains. It's common to see them gathered near gas or oil tanks in Wyoming; by transformer sheds along remote railways; hanging about Montana missile silos — grazing, chewing a cud, or simply sitting there measuring, sizing up these newcomer things. The pronghorn presence feels antecedent, way above all that, like the cockroach and the ginkgo.

As part of the human weathering, festering, of this country, sage, a holy substance a hundred years ago and still that for a tiny minority, has been cast by the present occupants, the rattlers of molecules, as an indicator of uranium deposits: Satellite photos suggest a connection between uranium lodes and particularly dense sagebrush growth.

From near the North Dakota border the struggle

between wheat cultivation and sagebrush intensifies. Suddenly there will be wheat everywhere, the tempo of the landscape different, subdued. Then the morphology roughens, breaks open. Hints of the badlands further downriver appear and the wheat fades. Back and forth it swings. North and east from Marmath, through the Little Missouri National Grasslands, flax fields show up, and then sunflowers, huge acreage of those docile yellow blooms—Blake *pekinoise*. West of Amidon I stop to pick a bundle of sage for the truck and put a big doublehandful of Great Northern beans to soak in a lidded coffee can. Back on U.S. 85, a few bikers buzz south.

The Missouri River where it cuts through the Dakotas has always been a major border, a demarcation between the heart of the high dry west and lower, moister things to the east. Oral traditions of most plains tribes retain at least a mythic notch at the point in their parched common past at which pedestrian ancestors crossed the Missouri from the northeast, maybe lingering for a generation before being forced or enticed on into a wandering life in the trans-Missouri country. A map of the upper Missouri shows the configuration: all the major tributaries leading south and west at regular intervals—the Knife, the Heart, the Cannonball, the Grand, the Moreau, the Cheyenne, the Bad, the White. . . . Access, avenues, inviting routes into the plains.

Some groups hit the Missouri and stayed. There

were people known as proto-Mandans on the North Dakota Missouri by 1000 A.D. Over the next 500 years other folks moved in, the Hidatsa joining the Mandans up here below the mouth of the Little Missouri and the Arikaras just over the line in South Dakota. They built earth homes on the valley terraces and grew corn and squash and beans and, like everyone else in the neighborhood, depended on the buffalo for meat.

Due to the combination of their fixed position and their successful agriculture yielding a surplus, the Missouri villages were soon vital trade centers, the most important hubs of commerce on the plains. Vegetable-hungry nomads wandered in by the tribe each year to trade dried meat and robes for corn. Some brought salt from the great salines down on the Arkansas. Quillwork and feathers were swapped for squash and beans. The upper Missouri villages were the only significant source of corn between the Mississippi valley and the garden plots of New Mexican pueblos. The same rivers that had led the nomads west from the Missouri handily took them back to trade.

About 1700, northern tribes brought English goods—guns, metal, cloth—from Hudson Bay and the plains peoples began driving in that new, revolutionary money, the horse, from New Mexico—the tendrils of those two widely separated European culture-extensions finally meeting, after decades of trade-carried rumors, at the Mandan villages. The following century the Missouri tribes saw Lewis and Clark,

Catlin, Bodmer, and Audubon, among others, come and go on the river.

The corn and other crops the village women tended, employing some of the essential dry-farm techniques (such as hoeing to retain soil moisture as much as to remove weeds) that later would be put to use by white settlers on the High Plains, were well attuned to the severe northern climate and eventually provided valuable genetic resources for European farmers' upper Missouri crops. The varieties of flint and flour corns were many, differing from tribe to tribe and village to village. Of 13 types of corn said to have been raised and carefully maintained as pure strains by the long ago Mandans, nine were in existence early this century. A total of 50 relatively pure corn strains have been preserved from the Missouri tribes. Typical yields have short 8 to 12 rowed ears. The names are a pleasure on the tongue: Ree pink; Arikara red; Omaha blue; Mandan soft yellow; Ponca gray; Pawnee red-speckle; Blackeye; Minniconjou purple. . . .

The women of the villages worked the scattered flood plain fields, hoed the corn, wooed it and sang to it, meticulously selected and stored their seed corn, danced for it spring and fall. The Mandan Goose Women Society held a ceremony at the sight of the first geese in spring, ritually offering dried meat to the returning flocks—all to make the year's corn grow, flourish, *come back*. In that annealed sense of the earth's processes "the geese and the corn were supposed to be one and the same thing."

Things fell apart quickly for the upper Missouri tribes. Vulnerable because of the fixed position that earlier had brought them wealth, they were devastated again and again after 1780 by smallpox and Sioux. Their population reduced by some 80%, the three tribes huddled together as one, finally, and were given a joint reservation at the mouth of the Little Missouri. There, ravaged almost to decimation, they regrouped on a fraction of the Missouri bottomlands their ancestors had lived and died upon for a thousand years. At least they had that, they said. But not for long.

A thousand year occupancy of any place on earth is so foreign a concept as to be incomprehensible to European settlers of this nation. It is a forgotten procedure, that continual crumbling into a humus that finally amounts to love. Descendants of pioneers speak stirringly of their land and form societies and haul the old machinery into the public parks after a curt three generations.

In the early 1950s the three tribes, after a thousand years as a bottomland people, were simply evacuated to make way for the Garrison Dam on the Missouri, which flooded a quarter of their reservation, including of course the best agricultural lowlands, the traditional village sites and burial grounds—the explicit land of their predecessors. "Ladies and gentlemen, this civilization is adjourned."

Now the Fort Berthold tribes are upland people, yanked 30 years ago up onto this rolling rangeland cut by coulees and thick with buffalo berry stands. From some of the reservation roads and from the hill

above the village of Mandaree the swollen Missouri—
the reservoir, "Lake Sakakawea"—is visible in
snatches. Here and there in magnificent relief and
hologram irony a red rototiller stands in a modest
patch of corn between an Indian home and the horse
herds at pasture.

I drove to the Snow Bird Cemetery to get out
and walk for a change and read the names on the
stones. A previous visitor had left a can of beer and
two packs of Salem Lights on the grave of relative or
friend. There was the grave of Henry Snow Bird,
1865–1956, the last man known to be born "on the
bottom," down in the last earth-lodge village, the
village called "Like a Fishhook." His stone holds a
laminated photo and a copy of his obituary. The
graveyard and chapel were named after him. "Snow
bird"—an old name for both the junco, a bird tending to the bottomlands in North Dakota winters, and
the snow bunting, an up-country grasslands-loving
winter visitor to the plains. A tiny node of unguent
in the language. . . .

Early this century there were Fort Berthold
Indians walking around with names like Adlai Steven-
son, Roscoe Conkling, and Oliver Twist. Given
names, as they say. During the land allotment days of
the latter 19th Century, the formal engraving of the
roll, white bureaucrats handed out European names
with a sniggering schoolboy humor. It was common
practice on dull days all over the west. The Wyoming
Arapahoes have had prominent Lincolns, Garfields,
Washingtons, and Grants, as well as a Cornelius Van-

derbilt and a William Shakespeare. The master German-silver worker of the southern plains was the Pawnee, recently dead, Julius Caesar.

H. L. Mencken describes the same procedure in a very different setting, Austria and Germany of the late 18th and early 19th Century, respectively, at which time native Jews were "compelled" to sign up, to assume official surnames. Those who balked or couldn't afford an adequate bribe were given names like Wanzenknicker (louse cracker) or Eselkopf (ass's head). For an interesting *fin de siècle* touch on the upper Missouri, there are records of an Arikara named Oscar Wilde by his boarding school supervisor, because of his haircut, no doubt, or a faraway Irish sort of look. In 1898 Mr. Wilde was petitioning to have his rightful family name restored.

It's a continual struggle in the west, as it is on much of the continent, to find even a shred of local traction, to come up with a material fragment evincing any day-to-day connection with its native ground. You must constantly force the issue, think it up, search it out, and track it down. In the case of food, that unflinching indicator of inner alignments, you often simply have to bring your own.

To gain a little footing, to dig in even a bit here at the Four Bears tribal park overlooking the Missouri, I get the coffee can of Great Northerns out of the pickup and put them on to boil. Great Northerns, the veal of beans—we ate them by the sweet cheap case in college—are a native upper Missouri bean, one of the handsome staples of the river people, and might well have fed Lewis and Clark. Great Northerns survived the cultural withering thanks to two men of vision. Late in the 1800s a Hidatsa man named Son of Star took a bag of Great Northern seed beans to a sympathetic horticulturist in Bismarck, a Mr. Will, and the strain was both registered and saved, soon to flourish. When I read that anecdote a few years ago I cancelled all appointments and took a long walk into the hills.

I chop a small onion and drop it into the beans with a toe of garlic. Big sturgeon-snouted clouds hang in the late afternoon sun, pointed east. The bluffs on the far shore of the Missouri, the village of Sanish, Crow Flies High Butte, all gently lit and held. Here and there in the park small groups of three-tribes people sit quietly overlooking the river, "the lake," with the same calm, grounded mien as the Navajos gazing out over their Canyon de Chelly.

I add a small can of corn to the beans, thinking to keep the meal as pure upper Missouri as possible, but in a few minutes I pull out a tin of Argentine corned beef and crumble it in. Beans will take it all, serve as ancient matrix for everything from baloney to chicken gizzards and beyond.

I eat them right from the pot with a squirt of tabasco. I eat them in a lawn chair with saltines and cold beer, watching the astounding light fade, then crawl into bed. Tomorrow I will transmit in the Great Northern tradition, I will be a carrier of the millenarian upper Missouri culture, farting softly in the streets of Bismark.

FOURTEEN

THE ROAD TO BILL

That winter-still Cheyenne River bottom, spidery as of charcoal sketch, haunts my dreams. North and west and east of Mule Creek Junction, Wyoming, time after time it rouses the blood in a way almost peculiar to that Thunder Basin and its headwater rivers, the Powder and the Little Powder, the Belle Fourche, the Little Missouri, the Cheyenne. East from Bill, north of Bill, the dirt roads north and east of Bill—whatever exactly it is, it is potent up there: unadorned curve of the earth.

Late fall even sagebrush takes on a new subdued tone, a hint of lavender burnish in the early sun. In May the Swainson's hawks are back in force from Venezuela, crisp and clean, joyriding the wind, one every mile. Summers, the dark gymnosperm green of the Pine Ridge—that textbook-clear upper edge of the High Plains, the long cedared descent into the Dakota systems visible to the southeast from north of Lusk—cools the eye. Midwinter there is the long insinuating beauty of a coal train with scores of new orange and black coal cars swaying east through the middle distance; or another, sitting quietly south of Bill, its rear end curling off and disappearing into low hills, the front half forming a quarter-mile wide perfect half circle as it waits beneath a desolate loading chute. The applied trigonometry of the tracks is the mathematical crystallization of the plains' snow-dusted latent curves.

It is, of course, partly size and scale. Hour on hour, rise after rise, it is the fugal space, coiling and repetitive, never outrun, never encircled or sucked dry. It is, accordingly, an unresolved landscape, a demanding one full of mock vacuum and suction and woo. You watch the land for signs and signals, for inflection, the way a sailor scans the sea, and for the words to size and fit them. There are rumples, crackles, and squalls of hills. There are flurries and flutters, bulges and swells. There is a salience, a shrug, a pizzicato. Chops and shoals. There are stillborn or baby bluffs, buds of buttes. Lips and flares, feints and fade-aways, yelp and bone and dimple.

Some days it is too much, some afternoons after six hours at the wheel, to find yourself out on the Thunder Basin. It is too much at once. The words go sour, never reach their referent. Futility and exhaustion rise through the body like fever. This is what they have called for a long time in the west *the Lonesome-ness*. It is a virulent form of vertigo laced with a cogent, planetary despair.

I have had trouble with it more than once up there near Bill, when it is all too much to keep up with, too big, even for the third or fourth time through; too big, too elastic, too strong. You have to stop the car and get out. The wind will be blowing, so take a coat or a blanket and walk off to the nearest arroyo or cut bank or gully. The sage will be quaking in the wind. If there are willow or chokecherry leaves ankle-deep in the place they will look disconcertingly like feathers.

Get down in there out of the wind and bundle up. Sit down, or lie down if you want, or roll like a dog in the sweet lee. Look at your boots, the buttons on your shirt, the burrs in your socks, anything near-at-hand and solid-edged. Prop on one elbow and fiddle with a stick in the dirt. Don't look up for a while. It is a hyperextension and a dislocation. It is an Ur-sadness in the Ur-scape. It is the cloth whipped out from under the set table. It is the despair of elemental isolation and simple limits, a sackbut sadness, the autumnal island sadness that illumines the gaunt Eliza-bethan tunes of Dowland and Morley and Byrd. You will close up like a flower closes for the night. You will sink and drift from the vertigo, falling gently until in a few minutes or half an hour you touch bottom and it is all restored in manageable scale. You hit bottom with the dull ventriloqual thud of deep sub-marines in the movies, alurk with their engines cut: *clunk*. Then you get up and stretch and walk back to the car.

Other mornings set their wings and sail. The four-state northern plains weather report in all its ex-travagant detail is intoxicating. The day and its space bring pure exaltation, the river bottoms easing into view a solid thrill: You know, amid the mock vacancy, that those trees were visited, that the spoor of humans is concentrated there, that down in the willows you have unarguable, though ghostly, company. For that reason even the grittiest creek bottom on the plains is stirring as a dream village from afar. No ruins neces-sary—a river like the Cheyenne is warm and famous and complicated in the distance as a city.

On the high days you are in the realm of the titans, mixing it up with the major components. Time

and Space meet out there on as visible and approach-
able a field as exists on the planet. They blend and
bump heads and interplay in new proportions with
new dynamics activated by automotive motion. They
meld and hybridize.

At this point we'll summon Monsieur Gaston
Bachelard and his airy treatise, *The Poetics of Space*:
"In its countless alveoli space contains compressed
time. That is what space is for." The man knows that
the deepest memories are most retrievable not through
time but through particular spatials via intimate solitude. Intimate solitude/intimate space is, for Bachelard, a house, a cubby, or a garret. The house is the
crucial place of daydream, revery, memory, all the
quiet restorative supra-individual currents of the idling
mind. As such a reservoir of daydream ("the original
contemplation"), the house is in this aspect alone of
major significance to the species. It is the bastion of
association and battery-charge unrivaled by out-of-
doors meditation.

When one transfers this enclosed capsule-like
frame of mind and all its potential from *house* to *car*
and then drives the car off across the plains northeast
of Bill, the result is a peculiar 20th Century phospho-
rescence. Automobiles have become as intimate and
laden with associations of security on this continent as
houses. I have dense early memories of the back seat
of my parents' Plymouth as I dozed after dark: the
smell of the heater, the low meandering talk, and the
flash and crawl of on-coming headlights. So the
mnemonic chemistry is the same, with an added vector.

It is revery in intimate motion, motion that somehow relieves time of its linear strain, replaces temporal-motion—that effort, that alignment or stacking of memory-data—with elemental space-motion. Time/Space yields to Motion/Space.

Automotive memory is a more fundamental, back-stroke sort of memory, a weightless, nonobligatory memory hatched in the car-capsule then blown out the window leaving a wake of tiny iridescent bubbles and a state of absolute buoyancy. You ride on an intimate earth, at home and unanchored at once. You are sprung into one of the more edifying species of joy.

There is the accumulative realization that the earth is a continually sensuous thing, out there where you can see it with minimal interference. Now this is a major grounding: The earth is active and mobile in as many-layered a way as to be expressive. The possibilities of Swedenborg's "The earth is human" unfold up between Bill and the Black Hills. Looks on the face, looks on the soft plains' scape. Subjunctive. Interrogative. A "raised eyebrow" off to the southwest.

That's what goes on up there on the upper reaches of the Cheyenne, the feeble reaches where it gathers its strength and form. Of all landscapes the open plain is the one of Possibility. Driving it is over and over a prow to ride, a cutting edge where fresh words surface and the mind is washed and hung. New inventions bubble up, new songs, new recipes, earth-moving speeches and revolutionary tools, as the husk splits open. Major projects, lavish gifts. . . .

I would like to drive Rilke around up there for a long day with a couple of Medocs and a strong cheese. I would like to set Gaston Bachelard down in a pup tent up there with a set of toy trucks or an electric train. And St. John Perse, the great conjurer of scenes, I would like to escort him on Highway 18 from Mule Creek to Edgemont and on south through Nebraska and Kansas to the Great Salt Plain on a fork of the Arkansas. We would climb a hummock there and conjure the great migrations to those flats in the old days, the camps and crowds, the gathering and packing of the salt in rawhide bags beneath a peony-clouded sky. That would make his heart sing.

Fifteen

The Edge of Wray

Where U.S. 34 crosses the North Republican a brown thrasher sings: multidimensional intersection and coordinate point of June crux potent as astrological gearage. To be born at this juncture bodes starry nights and puckered lips in chokecherry time. . . .

And in the cafe we have a whistler, a waitress lightly possessed, warbling along with the kitchen radio in sporadic but regular semi-automatic strains of some merit. "Send Me the Pillow" sort of stuff, a bit too loud and a bit too automatic, but a whistler nonetheless, quick with the coffee. She modulates above a nearby story of a traveling salesman offering a waitress down the road 65 thousand dollars to ride with him for a year and I remember as I listen a gifted whistler mailman in my hometown; how we heard him—a man otherwise shy, a man with a notorious *funny* brother—approaching in mid-morning a maple-shaded block or more away; the simple, no doubt inherited virtuosity of his public music, and how for years it oxygenated and faintly changed the cast of the town.

Sixteen

From Wolf Creek

count more than a dozen historic fort sites marked
on the road atlas for the Dakotas alone. There is, as
well, the world's tallest structure, the KTHI-TV tower
(2,063 feet) south of Mayville, N.D. Glancing over
the plains states there are the small red squares at the
usual hot springs and immigrant trails, battles and
treaties, the Cherokee Strip museum, the landing site
of a stratosphere balloon in the 1930s, natural oddities
and burial sites: value indicators on a collective bird's
eye view. There are scores more out there, half-lost
buoys in the workaday that rarely make the maps.

They have covered things pretty well, the stone
raisers. I have a fuzzy, no doubt dream-induced
"memory" of a Charles Starkweather monument somewhere in Wyoming; beyond the sign a set of snarling
tire ruts swerve nastily off into the sagebrush.

They are replacing the highway bridge over Wolf
Creek at the edge of Fort Supply, Oklahoma. The
water is temporarily rechanneled through a large cul-
vert below the makeshift detour crossing. The flow is
red, roily, and confused. Earthmovers and jackhammers
roar in the mess.

The early summer heat and its light haze are
distinctly southern. Just west, a state mental hospital
sprawls in spacious Hollywood grounds. A stately
half-mile double colonnade of shade trees borders the
gently curving entrance drive, over which orioles
twerp and sing. Pairs of dragonflies locked in mid-air
love hover, hang, and fade on the breeze.

In the spring of 1838 a large party of Cheyennes moved south from the Cimarron and surprised a Kiowa camp on Wolf Creek two or three miles northeast of here. An all-day hither and yon fight ensued — another dusty story, another vagueness, the general description of which can be found in half a dozen books. But George Bent, a gifted Cheyenne halfbreed, gives us in his letters a single zoom-focus buoyant detail, a fact transmitted by word of mouth for several generations until it hit the printed page: The first wave of the attack into the bottomland timbers caught many young Kiowa couples making love in the new spring underbrush. These comprised many of the early casualties that warm morning.

This detail, this discovery, this *pang* amid the gloss, rescued by a single sentence from utter oblivion, crystallizes this landscape, heightens the day and pigments the Wolf Creek water and gets me up in the back of the pickup to look downstream as far as I am able.

And what size hunk of rough granite could be hauled down there and left in memory of those lovers? What shape and cut and color? What weight in fitting proportion to the human ballast in the Wolf Creek groves?

It is a relict little tune, a fragment barely alive, but it plays about a pile of rubble and highwater debris in the low willows where the water breaks its banks some springs. Its musical lode is the indigenous howl and blues of the old continent, a bulldog blues reaching deep into the same gritty matter as the Mississippi

guitarmen and beyond into the untamed cries and calls
of wordless music. You can hear it in the old Sioux
and Comanche and Cheyenne peyote songs when they
leave the ground and the pitch rises along with the
hair on the nape of the neck.

The Fort Supply reservoir is choppy, blue-gray.
Cars and pickups sit in hot organized silence in the
hospital lot. Two patients or staff members throw a
day-glo tennis ball back and forth in the yard. And
there, there on the hillside above is the key, the verbal
linkage of the world that codes and interlocks it all:

*Patches of yellow locoweed toss in the blustery
wind.*

Seventeen

The Road to Circle

t's 41 degrees in Cut Bank, Montana. Four-day-old snowmen droop on the front lawns though it's hardly mid-September. Lap dogs yap from behind steamy windows as I stroll the early sidewalks. There are plastic tarps on the Cut Bank tomato plants and goose bumps on the cheerleaders' legs as they hurry to school in teams.

Down Main Street—U.S. 2, the north-scented "Highline," Puget Sound to Sault Ste. Marie and beyond—neon from the cafes shines through mist. Cut Bank is, among other things, a northernmost extension of the biscuits and gravy line, one of the few places to find them north of the Yellowstone River.

It is the first grayness and the first moist chill of the year, for me. It is a morning of huddling and of *things*. Things in store windows; unattended things; things lent a delicate aura this season of any year. Cheap shoes with a three month life expectancy, kids' clothing from Taiwan, footballs that explode on first punt—the temperature, the slide from summer, sets them all in a tenuous context, fleshes them out, adds a poignancy factor. Things that would look tacky in Oklahoma or in July stand out clearly, illuminated by their simple latent usefulness, by their niche of conception/execution, in Cut Bank September.

Hardwares and dimestores are richest. I spend ten minutes in front of the archery gear, assorted wheelbarrows, a rack of cast iron skillets. This is a moment of sympathy for Uncle Earl Long of Louisiana, who, they say, on certain days bought up irrational quantities of almost anything (a dozen and a half post-hole diggers at a clip, to name one example), swept away by the magnetics and fresh paint of the human object. . . . Even the electric cattle prods are lovely this morning.

Over on Railway Street near the grain elevators a massive, extra-fancy maroon Peterbilt semi idles steadily, the driver apparently napping in the big red-curtained rack until business gets moving. On the sleeper door there is a delectable schematic of a map, a haiku-like diagram of an alluring route that would make a slick tattoo: the Houston to Edmonton, Alberta, run.

The entire day was locked in under a gray quilting of cloud. East from Cut Bank on the Highline. Beyond Shelby the snowy flanks of the Sweetgrass Hills were just discernable beneath the clouds to the north, but generally the visibility was low, the spatials were gone, there was nothing but the near-at-hand, the ever-present railroad tracks along the road, sections of Burlington Northern or Soo Line cars standing at ease, or the occasional missile silo to dispel any romantic nonsense. For Montana, it was like being indoors.

In one small village—it might have been Chester—a custom threshing crew was organizing and loading up in the half-drizzle, making convoy to head south for the year. Big combines inched around corners; Illinois, Oklahoma plates.

In Havre I toasted the Glacier Motel, an old yellow and brown ramshackle complex that archaeologists may well take for a fort or a turkey ranch. I

stayed there a year ago to the roar of Highline trucks.
My hotplate dinner—browning the stew beef in
Crisco—set off the smoke alarm. The torn-down Ford
Fairlane with something like day-glo green fishnet
spilling out of the trunk over by room 23 hasn't
moved in 12 months.

From Havre east I have Milk River to pass my
time, snatches of its cottonwoods drifting from one
side of the highway to the other, some 175 miles of it.
It changes everything, we're suddenly riverine, it leads
and validates the way with its implicit gradient,
steady as a coastline.

Approaching Wolf Point I meet the stubby west-
bound "Empire Builder" en route from Chicago to
Seattle. In town I take a room at the Tip Top. The
owners' son, I learn, is the star quarterback of the
Wolf Point High School team. The whole family is
ready to set out for Circle, the opponent of the
evening, 52 miles south. I borrow their portable radio
to follow the game in my room; set up the hotplate,
pull out the George Dickel, and get comfortable,
"happy as with a woman."

The game, what 25% of it I could decipher, is a
lopsided Wolf Point smear. The duo of local an-
nouncers are inept enough in a perversely synchronized
way to cancel each other out most of the time. It is,
understandably, a soggy game. There is a melee early
in the second half, followed by the ejection of the
beleaguered Circle quarterback, who is replaced, if I
got it right, by the left guard. He seems to improve
things for the home team, but not much.

All night a rackety Canadian wind shook the
motel. By daybreak the heavy cloud cover is gone.
It's all jammed up on the southern horizon I discover
when I cross the Missouri and head south, climbing
the Yellowstone-Missouri divide, up into the high and
heady. I've got a tailwind the hawks love; the road is
rollicking and free-form up here away from the dic-
tates of rivers and it's all mine this morning. The
isolate houses and churches are rigorous rectangles,
white clapboard with stubborn red trim. It's a stark,
depot sort of architecture, broken now and then by a
blue-green shed, lonesome and newspaper caulked as
upper Quebec or outer Saskatchewan. Lark flocks
rise from the shoulder to be blown south-southeast en
masse—migration by the scruff of the neck.

I round a long curve and come upon a herd of
handsome unknown cattle in a low pocket meadow
sporting a scraggly willow patch. A herd so striking and
uniform that I pull over and put the binoculars on
them. They are glossy black, sturdy beef animals with
wide white girdles circling their midsections. Two dozen
or so, virtually identical in color and form, all now
watching me, their ears perked, chewing suspended,
on the verge of an expectant step in my direction.

It's a moment for applause. They are a tableau
to kith and kin and speciation, that endless branching
of the flower. I watch them the way I watched thousands of sandhill cranes the first time in the Platte
valley: wave after wave of identical birds coasting in
low over the road, skein after skein, two-thirds of the
world's population. Species, genus, genes in their

pools—all those terms were immediately clear, hammered in the March air by a thousand crane calls.

These unknown cattle in their tight herd raise the same hackles in a quiet bovine way. After days of nothing but angus these new creatures are a visual treat and a flare.

I learned later they were Belted Galloways from Scotland, an old breed valued by Scottish drovers in centuries past for their high visibility on dark foggy days, one of a dozen Old World breeds that have freshened the American gene pools since 1960, cattle of remarkable pedigree and pasts, like the French Limousins, probable descendants of the Lascaux cave bulls; the Italian Chianinas, one of the oldest and largest breeds in the world, tracing lineage to pre-Roman Empire Tuscany's Chiana Valley, home of the Chiantis; the dark-cherry red Salers from central France, thought to be descended from the ancient Egyptian "red cattle"; the South Devons (the "gentle giants") and the pinto Maine-Anjous; Pinzgauers from Salzburg; and from the Pyrenees the honey-colored breed I would drive far to see, the Blonde d'Aquitaines.

I leave the Belties—they have restored my faith in things international and ancient—and drive on. Twenty minutes later I'm in Circle.

Circle is *up there* and *out there*. I drive slowly through town and run a quick stitch-loop to the football field, set lightly amid sagebrush a mile south of town.

Nothing much moving in Circle. It's 8 A.M. Saturday. All the players sleep on.

EIGHTEEN

The thought of certain lives can lead one to break two-by-fours.

North and a little west of Red Cloud, Nebraska, on the rolling Republican-Little Blue divide, there stands an empty farmhouse preserved as the fictional home of Tony Shimerda/Cuzak in Willa Cather's *My Antonia*. When the weather has been wet the farmstead is a half-mile walk down a greasy gumbo road from the nearest all-weather. It is a good way to approach the place. From behind the dense shelter belt a chunky white frame house slowly emerges. Remnants of March snow hang in the roof angles. Then a big tin barn behind it; a shed or two. Closer, the barnyard has a recently abandoned look, a preserved look. A superannuated farm truck moulders under a tree.

There is a complete, precarious stillness about the place, a curious silence beyond the chatter and bicker of house sparrows in shrubs down by the barn and ponds. Day-old coon tracks skirt the leafless windrow. An old fruit tree stump, cut off four feet above the ground, is bushy with new growth. Fifty feet from the house the cellar door juts from the earth — the cellar door leading to barrels of pickled watermelon rind in the novel, the door that pours forth Antonia's brood in a sun-drenched *moment fixe*.

The gray day seeps and slops. The layers of the place, the fact/fiction relationship, the play between the fictitious Antonia and the Pavelka girl, her prototype who lived here, broke the tall-grass sod — all this makes for an evasive, almost eerie suspension. The lines of a life, as on a palm. The luminous, slow-

moving spot of a life, the land it stands upon, and
the artful act that crystallizes it into stories of the
great complex ecology.

What leavens Willa Cather's prairie books is the
elementary unmistakable secret of all books that send
one to the two-by-fours: Behind the fiction there is
the actual referent, a detail-studded ballast from a real
and long-absorbed world. The light on the sandbars
of the Republican River. The roll of the red-grass
landscape. It is an imagination of heightening and ar-
ranging a given world rather than one of aggressive
invention. Its eyes are soft but sharply focused. It picks
up small things and turns them slowly in the hand.
Bee-bush and rose mallow; ruts of old roadways. The
colors are primary and fast.

So we are given a human life incandescent in its
arc, an Antonia of heartbreak and blossom, or the
fated lovers beneath an apple tree in *O Pioneers*. And
the galvanic thoughts of their various actual vectors
are nearly matched in intensity by thoughts of the
warm gifted eye that saw it all and chose it, and the
cool lean prose that set it down amid the manifold
flows and currents of the daily species. Here at this
house the process and the spark of it all are nearly
tangible. A human life and a sharp pencil. The sharper
the pencil the finer the line, the sparer the accompa-
niment, the higher the solo parts. And the life stands
out then, as the act of noticing stands out, in its passion and cartilege through the fine tracery of its line.

We circle the house, leaving soggy footprints in
the spotty snow, shading the eyes against the window

glass to peer in the empty rooms. A small stairway;
the kitchen and its pump. Fragrant ghosts of Tony's
spiced plum kolaches.

Earlier today we had circled and peeked in the
same restless, hungry way through the lace curtains
of the Cather childhood home in Red Cloud. Tomorrow we will do likewise at the wind-blasted concrete
block Mari Sandoz museum farther west, near her
birthplace in the Sandhill solitude: a handful of dusty
personal items, a strange unidentified naked manni-
kin, Mari's large wall map of Manhattan far from her
Hudson Street apartment, a few sharp pencils.

Layers and echoes and the still farmhouse of a
Bohemian family fictive as unicorns, carved out of
the Republican valley and blown off the palm of the
hand like cottonwood fluff. And "that is happiness,
to be dissolved into something complete and great."
And this raw day of the ankle-deep mud the Hastings,
Nebraska, phonebook is full of Pavelkas.

Driving northwest from Red Cloud it is possible
to cross the Platte River (known in the early 1800s as
the Nebraska, its roughening valley to the west called
the Coasts of Nebraska, as in *côtes*) at about the
same moment one crosses the 99th meridian, that
hypothetical divider of East from West representing
the continually wavering, wandering moisture line
that separates prairie from plain—during the drought
of the 1930s it crept 100 miles eastward.

Biologically, the plains have usually been viewed
as a sort of negative space, divisive space defining and

enforcing the continent's east-west speciation. Eastern flora/fauna mingle with the western in ragged overlap as the former creep up the river valleys in their farthest extensions. Climbing north from the Platte and west from the 99th, there are distinctions on the human level as well. This is the ascent from the *hither* to the *yon*, from farm to ranch, tillage to herding. The change is one of attitude and mentality; almost of viscosity. From the massively irrigated, utterly possessed Platte valley one climbs through Custer County to the Loup divide through an unrelenting, musical progression of rises and falls, ascending steadily into the open and the roofless, to the great Sargasso of the plains, the Sandhills.

Of all the geographical pockets on the continent, the Sandhills and their sheer rippling extent hang in the mind like clouds seen from a plane above. Their 20,000 square miles comprise the largest sand dune area in the western hemisphere. They remain the "greatest unbroken grassland in North America." They are among the great cattle producing regions in the world. As pure wilderness—in the sense of untrammeled and self-willed space—the Sandhills hold their own against any mountain terrain.

Lying between the Platte and the Niobrara rivers, the hills were formed thousands of years back when mighty winds from the north stirred ancient river beds and piled their sands into long parallel dunes. Big ones extend 10 miles and loom 350 feet high. The dunes are stabilized by thrifty bunchgrasses, but within the system there is continual change as wind and

other disturbances to the fragile surface alter the lay
of the dunes. The result is a rolling, billowing, delicate
landscape unique in the west. Approaching from
Broken Bow, or Gordon, or Ogallala, once you top
the first real hill and drop into this utterly different
topography with its more complicated spatials, something closes behind you and the earth feels possible
and receptive again.

From high points you see them ripple away, the
hills, mile upon mile, muscular yet gentle, supple but
spartan. Wind-rumpled, pocked and dimpled. Dream
mountains. It is a reassuring spaciousness (the Sandhill population density must rival outer Nevada's)
surrounding the elemental rhythm of the ranches as
one moves from water-wealthy hay meadows resting
close upon the Ogallala aquifer to yucca-dotted
grazing reaches. It is a place one can drive happily in
circles for days.

The hills also muster some of the harshest living
conditions in the world. The wind is a constant and
in winter brings slashing blizzards and a mineral
cold. Summers, it can whip fires for miles through
the dry grasses; you can smell a Black Hills blaze way
down in Cherry County, Nebraska.

From a friend's cottonwood-shaded ranch house
north of Hyannis I hike north over the first range of
hills. George, the bull-chested tireless black mutt,
comes along. It's a midsummer day; the going is slow
in the sand. Sharp-tailed grouse flush off as we get
higher in the yucca and rosehips, or are suddenly there

cackling and coasting over a rise. Up-wind half a mile three mule deer stare and ease off into the dunes. In a small blow-out—one of those cups of vegetationless sand common in the hills—an unexpected resident stops everything to crane at me: a box turtle, one of many I would see that day, all of them plowing their way across blow-outs. As I kneel beside him I picture him reaching out for a rosehip in astounding slow motion, grasping it just right in his beak.

Coyotes yap and whine regularly even though it's mid-morning by now. There is a cut-off distance to which George the tireless is carefully attuned. If the coyote is within that range George is off like a shot toward it across a meadow and over a rise at least a half mile distant. Thirty seconds later he reappears and races back to me, never slackening the only pace he knows. If another coyote cuts loose in the other direction ten seconds later George is off again without a thought. Now and then he pauses to work a cactus needle out of his foot, but in general his energy and sense of limits are boundless and staggering.

From the top of a good hill, I watch valley, range, valley roll away, receding infinitely like the images in a barber's mirrors. This part of Cherry County is within the "lake country" and nearly each valley is graced with a chain of long narrow lakes from three to six feet deep. I can see four lakes in two different valleys to the north. This sweet water drew men of the Dismal River culture centuries ago. This morning's breakfast was built around a platter of fried Sandhill bullheads and a pile of biscuits to wash down the bones.

To the untrained eye all these valleys look the same. Early mustangers in the hills were forced to haul in tall poles from the Dismal to place atop certain hills as landmarks. George and I descend on a slalom angle to the nearest lake. Bullrushes grow thick along the shore; on the far side I find a muddy little beach covered with duck droppings and scattered feathers. Cicadas drone and marsh wrens rattle from the rushes. I am as alone as I have been in a long, long time. The noon is hot and the deerflies and "greenheads" are biting with vengeance. There is no human sign visible or audible, save a fenceline trailing up and over the hills nearby. The heat, the expansive silence, and the cluttered mud on that shore, stirred by a lethargic intermittent breeze, concoct a primeval feeling. I sit there amid the duck scat for half an hour, then strip down and wade in for a neolithic splash and swim.

To swim alone, completely alone in the middle of many hectares, is a luxuriant thing. Maxim Gorky wrote five interesting pages on "Man's Behavior When Alone." Chekhov stubbornly pursuing a sunbeam with his hat. Tolstoy whispering confidentially to a lizard on a wall—men for whom solitude was a rare circumstance. In the Sandhills it is sometimes the dominant commodity.

On another trip to Cherry County we stopped to visit a friend of the family, an 80-year-old bachelor rancher living alone a mile off a tertiary half-road in a place that throbbed with that open-ended, one-way silence of isolation. We found him sitting at the kitchen table mending his leather work gloves with an awl and cobbler's needle, mending the gloves he would need to mend his fences. His house dated from the 1960s; the original homestead stood a few yards away. He had framed arrowheads and photos of nieces on the walls. There was a huge television in one corner. He rose to the sudden occasion of company by reeling off old stories and Sandhill jokes laced with family references and national politicians. It was all in the vein of a child's piano recital, somehow, in its pure desire to please.

Outside, he showed us the old thick-walled sod home where he was born and reared. It stands full of junk and racoon droppings. And then we all shook hands and said goodbye. There was an almost audible clicking off of the social in the man's carriage and eyes. It was a small Sandhills epiphany. I glanced back as we pulled away and saw him walking, a bit stiffly, even formally, back inside, alone again, for how many days?

George and I while away three hours by the lake, working the rushes for a clear view of the wrens, slapping greenheads and taking occasional dips. We are visited by several dazzling red damselflies; I should collect one for a still-life painter. Now and then a night hawk dives and roars overhead, that most ethereal, unplaceable sound from above that never fails to excite and baffle the dog. A trio of white pelicans flies with great dignity across the far end of the lake. It's time to dress and pack up and head over the hills. As we climb away south, the light is just changing, fading toward sundown, and a summer moon is low

on the hills. Away down below, young night herons
flop along shore in that reduced golden glow—the
delicate re-mix of two celestial lights—and a huge
solitary angus bull stands chewing his cud in knee-high
grass to the west end of the valley.

The Sandhills are as private as the Ozarks.
Children frequently commute 60 miles a day to school,
or board in town during the week. As is typical of
areas where human company is valued for its scarcity,
news travels fast, people know one another for 50
miles in all directions, and their recall of events past
is phenomenal. Around the dinner table or sipping
whiskey in the bunk house, they reach back and pull
them in with casual dexterity.

"I worked for him in the hayfields in 1929."

"I never got to North Platte till '54."

"We were at a rodeo up in White River in '47."

"I bought that mower in the spring of '68."

Regarding the infamous blizzard of 1949, I heard
a rancher recite the full name of the man who drove
the National Guard bulldozer that finally showed up
days after to clear the ranch road, how they saw the
blinking lights moving slowly toward them down
the valley, the name of the man who sat beside him,
who he had married, when, and the name of the boy
who drove the fuel truck following behind.

—When the railroad pushed west from Broken Bow
into the hills, someone among the crew was a Massachusetts man with a good eye. Moving through the
dunes he aptly named a village Hyannis. There is also

a Whitman, and farther south in Nebraska, a Wellfleet.
With the railroad providing a ready outlet the cattle
business boomed in the Sandhills and big-time ranchers
prospered. Many bought shady town homes in
Hyannis and retired there. In 1931 the Omaha *World-
Herald* called Hyannis (present population 360) "the
richest town in America." In 1947 the *Saturday
Evening Post* described it as the "Sand Hills Paradise,"
"the town with 13 millionaires."

Today, coal trains lumber east through the village
twice or three times an hour carrying low-sulfur coal
from Wyoming. They lumber by the spot where Teddy
Roosevelt stopped for a tailgate moment during one
of his campaigns, past the local fur buyer with his
ancient trailer full of dried coyote hides, past the millionaires' modest frame homes. But when I stroll along
those tracks or follow them east or west on Highway 2,
I find myself thinking of a different Sandhills visitor.

In mid-1943 Fort Robinson, an old military
installation northwest of the hills near the South Dakota line, was designated a POW camp, one of several
in Nebraska; one of many in the heartland. All the
western camps were under the supervision of the largest
facility near Atlanta, Nebraska, south of the Platte.
The Atlanta camp processed some ten thousand German prisoners during its two-year existence. Prisoners
from the North African theater, mostly—Rommel's
men, arriving on slow trains from the east coast,
destined for casual farm labor and irrigation work in
the surrounding countryside.

Fort Rob was a smaller satellite, processing only

1500 men during the late war. It was a typical camp with three compounds within a barbed wire stockade, guard towers, and machine guns. All this within yards of the log jail where Crazy Horse was killed in 1877 and the stockades where Dull Knife's Cheyennes were held and later shot down escaping one freezing January night. Nights in the mid-40s you might have heard *biergarten* tuba tunes drifting from the compounds to the Red Cloud bluffs.

In the spring of 1945, one German soldier simply walked away from a work detail and hopped a freight on the Burlington line. It carried him south from Crawford to Alliance, then east through the heart of the Sandhills: Ellsworth, Hyannis, Thedford, and southeast through Grand Island. After dark the man detrained in York, Nebraska. His priorities were admirable. He cavalierly entered a joint called "Buddy's" and even more cavalierly ordered *eine bier*. Back at Fort Rob the next day, he explained he wanted to see America; especially Omaha.

Now, at least once each trip to the Sandhills, at some heady point on the highway when the big spaces re-open in the head and the heart, I think of that man and his day through these hills many Americans don't know exist. Some of the Nebraska POWs returned to the state to farm after the war. Maybe the escapee is here somewhere, taking it easy in Omaha or rocking away on a Sandhills porch by now. Either way, I see him 40 years ago crouched in the door of an empty freight car lumbering through the hills, peeking out full of adrenalin-spiked wonder.

Nineteen

South of Riverton I stop and turn back for a sage
grouse dead beside the road. Someone's been there
before me—all the tail feathers neatly plucked: We
have entered a Culture Area.

Hollyhocks are blooming in the Wind River
country. A red and white—peppermint—combination
stands out in the chill morning. "Bill Budd for
Governor" signs curl on telephone poles—(some elfish
Dance of the Names while everyone's sleeping). Two
sandhill cranes glean grain in the Little Wind Valley,
look up tall when I honk.

I give Mr. Lauren Shakespeare a brief lift, stop
and turn back to check what seems to be the slender
wing of a struck falcon lilting in the berm grass. It's
a cashed-in, off-course gull.

TWENTY

WRITING ON STONE

The culinary specialties of the Canadian Great Plains are butter tarts—pocket sized pies filled with toothsome honey-raisin fillings—and, at a discreet interval, dill-pickle flavored potato chips.

———————

At Writing-on-Stone, that gifted place on Milk River where "the rocks come out of the ground," by the simple fact that we are in Canada by 25 miles we find ourselves facing north a good bit of the time. This narrow valley with its sculpted maze of sandstone hoodoos is a fitting place to close the eyes and think of the northern edge, the ragged intermittent edge of the grasslands. It is nourishing exercise to follow the edge in the mind all the way around the plains; but the northern one is the most anonymous, most remote and insulated by its border of dense bush and forest-lands.

Last year we went up to see it, to find and follow it for a while. We started from this place on Milk River, then, and drove to Medicine Hat ("the Hat"), where gulls' cries mix curiously with magpies' over the downtown in early morning. Through the Cypress Hills, from whose high wildflower meadows you might flash mirror signals a long, long way; to Saskatoon, the city named after a berry, its unruly sundown sky; to the forks of the Saskatchewan River. And there is pretty much where you begin to sense the edge, the first scraggly upstart hum of the bush country, Cree country, and swing west along it.

The farther north one goes in Alberta the more

Chinese food prevails. There is plenty in Edmonton, a city I would like to nose around for several days, and by the time you hit Peace River and Grimshaw (where we finally turned south) there is little else but drive-ins with menus of 50 far-removed Chinese platters and a few milkshakes.

But that stretch west and north from the forks of the Saskatchewan was a demarcation, the break-out point from countless acres of wild forest and black flies to the open and the unimpeded. There is a constant sense of emergence, skirting that edge, a feeling of continual stepping forth out of the bush to unfold in an immense new cyclorama.

To imagine a collective ancestral mouth dropped open at that juncture was the assignment that week, as its human signature, the image that sticks by virtue of its silhouette and thrift, is one from a campground near Vermilion, Alberta, an edgey place with hordes of mosquitos and scattered popple. We were neighbors to an extended ranch family on holiday. I had gone off to pick a double handful of Saskatoons. When I returned, four men and boys were warming to an old, slender, north-country version of nine pins on the mowed campground grass, using three empty pop bottles and a shabby softball. It was unmistakably a game they saved for special family occasions and it held the imagination with its flint-and-steel simplicity. They went at it slow and steady for half an hour while the women readied supper. Those bottles and that grass-stained ball would have graced a minor spotlight in any museum.

The Writings on the Stones here along Milk River have been pecked and scratched low on the sandstone hoodoos by many generations of various peoples. "What I am"; "What I did." They are understated and eloquent as the radio message-plaques cast into far space by our own day bearing a schematized human hand. Inscriptions run from very old and essential stick figures with large round shields to later mounted men to "Doug '79." The hoodoo stretch of the valley, several miles in extent, was a significant place for early Shoshonean peoples, Cree and Blackfoot visitors: Big rains still wash offering beads from hoodoo crevices.

It's latter afternoon at the moment and mule deer are showing up on the hilltops above the river, above the creamy gold of the sandstone formations, waiting to descend for their evening drink and browse in the bottomlands. The thick stands of Wolf Willow and buffaloberry are full of mixed sparrow flocks skittery with a latitudinal autumn now in August. A cock pheasant cackles downstream and a droning that must be a farm truck on Highway 501 five miles north goes on for what seems 20 minutes, like a lazy jet. Shortly I'll dig out the two-volume Random House Proust— an old battered set from college, ex libris one Alma Krauss—and do my exercises while potatoes and onions roast in the coals.

From beyond the barrier of shrubs northern voices wander in, voices with that clipped, long-vowelled, tenor, semi-interrogative accent of the 49th parallel. It

is an ingratiating accent, readily absorbed. I have a
friend, a notorious osmotic, who will show up after a
long transcontinental tour with a subtle farrago of
dialects and accents—Maine, Carolina, Texas—by
which we can reconstruct his trip linguistically the way
scholars trace the migration of the ancient gypsies
from Asia through the middle east and Europe, a jour-
ney of centuries, by the diverse root syntax of their
eventual New Romany tongue as spoken in England.

It is a sensitive relationship, that between the ear
and the tongue, one susceptible to tropisms and
atmospheric pressures of all kinds. A solo week on
the High Plains can work major linguistic shakedowns.
Those driving days of relative isolation and asocial
silence sift the language into new or forgotten old
formations. The alternate, transactional voices will
slough off, the ventriloqual will shrivel and drop away.
After a few days the language-pack will reduce and
clarify itself to the point that it is palpably there, like
oxygen tanks on a diver. The vocabulary is rested,
reshuffled, and shined; the syntax relaxed and coiled.
You pull up at a gas station for the first human inter-
course in ten hours and speak well marbled unmistakable words.

Often they will be words from deep in the speech
beds, old words from the fossil-rich layers of first
childhood absorption with its eccentricities of application and tiny but ineradicable pronunciation miscues,
up through the social-educational amplification of
vocabulary and the heady extent of its music and variety and power, from the thousand books and bom-

bardment by the thousand voices. It is a dense soil, but one day given motion and silence the old words will surface, bob up and shine, and you will, if necessary, go out and seek someone to use them on after a long non-vocal afternoon—stop at a store for something you hardly need in order to speak a word or two your mother used 30 years ago. . . . *Wapper-jawed. Hellion. Stem to gudgeon.*

You can detect early on in people's faces and in their speech whether their past is intact, whether they are even aware of their speech beds. Those prairie bowlers, lank men and their lank boys, likely had vocabularies hardly disturbed since childhood. Proust, a great aural archeologist, had an ear as full and sensitive as the best of eyes. He relished the speech layers of his characters again and again, from the telling regional intonations of the beach girls to the shard-laced speech of Madame de Guermantes with its trace elements of ancient nobles under the trees—a speech as level, wealthy, and gently leashed as an old song.

To hear with that amazing depth of understanding, even once to realize the reverberations and source of a companion's words, enhances the act of speech forever, enriches the verb. It is no longer simply *to speak*; the tongue is more active than that. In a real sense, for a moment there when, knowingly and partakingly, we speak from that lingual main channel, we are also *spoken*.

As for this writing on paper, it leaves a pencil callous high on the inner middle finger. The words come out of the pencil here at the picnic table the way "the rocks come out of the ground." Writing on paper settles the words, one's own herd of them and their inner world and outer blossoms. It is an arrangement.

Here among the drawings and scratchings I wanted to write a few hundred words in the same context, just the one, the head-high markings: To line up as at the blackboard for the daily writing, to take one's place for a minute, then dip in the Milk. To do it as the stationmaster posts his schedules and the cook puts up his daily specials on the fresh-wiped chalkboard—"Cod Chowder," "Chicken Heart Chili"—Writing on stone.

TWENTY-ONE

n Miles City early one morning I examined, and should
have sketched or traced or photographed, a dense
oblong scramble of black rubber marks an inch and a
half wide and 12 feet long where elementary boys
race and skid their bikes—*power slide*—on the concrete
apron of a parking lot again and again, leaving two-
tone compositions Pollock-like in their insistence and
tangle and implications.

In Gillette, Wyoming, in Fort Benton, Montana,
in Elkhart, Kansas, the young men drive the strips
for hours, goosing their engines, squalling tires, leaning on horns, cruising in rectangular loops, vicious
would-be circles, tracing and retracing the same route
all evening, craning their necks and gaping at pedestrians, cracking their mufflers, as locked in their drive
mechanism as any April prairie chicken.

These are hardly Great Plains phenomena; out
here their noise simply carries farther. Their dull
automotive tracer-circles and their resonance stand out
more clearly and more absurdly than in Tennessee or
California. The commonest thing is enunciated by the
hunkering tactile night—*power night*.

The violence that lurks and erupts on the plains
in its present forms, echoes of the brutality and
adrenalin that took them, that has always taken them
and everywhere else on earth and holds them each day
and night, is the product of vacuity, of space and the
ego-sonar rippling off in widening concentric circles
with no reply, with nothing to bounce off. Without
some other, inner frame of reference, some instilled
sense of anchor and identity, this life without echo

builds angry frustration the same way some city life forms lava through the opposite process: the continual jamming of the sonar by social density. Both lead to a ferment of melancholy, brooding hatred, and occasional murder.

Some days we feel it—the brutality of emptiness—in the towns and the two-dimensional strips and brittle bars so strong that we drive to the nearest Indian land to see other faces. God knows Indians have their own passionate violence and frustrations and murder, but it is different when it wells; it is not worn on the upper lip or in the everyday t-shirt pocket; it doesn't permeate the very air or embarrass the vegetation or freeze the very meat of the faces with the viral cheapness of its cause.

One sundown in Gillette, the energy boomtown that tripled in size within several years, drawing sociologists in hordes, we saw, in an unforgettable synchronization, both displays at once. The big mud-caked souped-up pickups loaded with drilling gear roared and boomed and whinnied up and down the drag by the score. On adjacent sidewalks the little schoolboys chased and screamed, spitting, yelling shrilly in groups of three or four under fast-food neon, turning power slides and pulling wheelies on their sawed-off bikes—a glittering socio-motor cameo by Bosch-light. A particular din hanging over its particular night town like fumes above a cauldron.

TWENTY-TWO

t is hard to lay hold of the Llano Estacado when you're up there on it. It is more of an entity, almost, from afar—from the Cimarron country to the north, from the Pecos to the west—when it hangs solid and sea-gray on the skyline.

It is even tricky to pin the Staked Plains down on maps, but in essence they extend south from the Canadian River through west Texas and adjoining New Mexico as far as the Pecos, comprising the most legendary cut of the Great Plains. They are the southern contingent of the High Plains and therefore they bulge, press upward, leaving you on a high and endlessly obvious central point. It is different, sensationally, from the Flats, for example, that stretch of mercilessly even country north from the Canadian 200 miles into southeast Colorado, considered by geographers to be the most level "upland feature" in the world. The Flats have a high swaddling horizon, an optical concavity, compared to the Llano.

The Staked Plains have always been a place to wander, for better or for worse, a formidable anti-maze of bleached bones, mirage, and the shortest grass on earth. Some say the name derived from early Spaniards leaving a Hansel and Gretel-type trail of inedible marker posts behind them as an exit option. For those who knew its inner workings the Llano's harsh dry loft made it a traditional place of refuge and sanctuary. The Kiowas fled to the Llano in desperation during the smallpox rage of 1839, hoping to outrun the fevers. They fled there again with the Comanches 30 years later hoping to outrun the soldiers, moving from secret waterhole to secret waterhole. It was the place to go after any frontal exposure to the heinous.

It is still hard to lay hold of. You might drive from Hereford to Clovis to Muleshoe to Tokio to Eunice and be not quite sure you're getting it, wonder a bit about those Staked Plains, that whip-cracked cotton and sorghum country going by. For a handle you might have to settle for half a dozen Mississippi kites hanging motionless high above some fortunate river town, which is the greatest of plenty, or call up that brooding image of the Llano from afar and keep it on the dashboard as you go.

Then turn eastward, and watch. Say from Bovina through Dimmit and Tulia and on. Over beyond Silverton you will hit the Caprock, the drop and bevel that defines the Llano at last, a theatrical canyoned edge that tumbles sharply to the prairie plains. A variant explanation of the adjective *staked* refers to the distant view of this edge, its sudden palisaded appearance. It is a feature prominent in the minds of men—there is Caprock Oil, Caprock Trucking, Caprock this and that. It is a definer and therefore an anchor.

Circle out through Turkey or Matador and head back to the Llano, now that you know what it is.

The winds on the Texas panhandle average 14 miles per hour, the highest in western America, a velocity on the par of outer Cape Cod and Cape Hatteras. They range from the blistering summer south winds that can curl a cornfield in two days to the fiercest blizzards. Even in their more temperate forms they are a major psychological presence with their constant hammering. They take a dry climate and dry it further. The evaporation rate from April to September ranges from 52 to 55 inches; in North Dakota it is about 30 inches for the same period.

From the beginning, European settlers attacked the water problem in Texas with alacrity and free-rein imagination. At the turn of the century one William Little suggested building a series of parallel wooden walls or tree-belts across the plains from Mexico to Canada to slow the winds. In the '90s, working on the ancient theory that "rain follows battles," high explosives were mustered in Texas under Department of Agriculture auspices to shake loose a storm or two. Three lines of fire were deployed, each two miles long, a half mile apart, consisting of ground batteries and high riding explosive balloons. Salvos were fired at hour intervals. Toward evening an encouraging cloud and a few scattered droplets were reported.

But it was the windmill that found its niche and blossomed on the plains, converting wind to water in one of the great alchemies. The American version—of collapsible metal, smaller and more manageable than its huge European ancestors—hit the plains in the 1870s, first in the company of the transcontinental rail-roads, providing regular water stations for locomotives, and was soon an emblem of the region, bringing cattle tank and patch of green and truck garden. Unlike the massive deep-pivot wells introduced in the 1950s, which threaten the deepest recesses of the Ogallala aquifer, windmills stand in good relation to their earth. They are sensible things and welcome landmarks. You can hear them rattling and clanging a long way off on the plains; from a sleeping bag at night it is a companionable aeolian sound. There are towns today on the Staked Plains where most homes have their own windmill in the yard; towns like Mt. Dora, New Mexico, with more Aeromotors than trees.

When I drive through farm country at harvest time I remember peasants in one of Tolstoy's books breaking from long hard work to a lunch of black bread and salted cucumbers in the shade of a haystack. The image has become a subliminal feature of that midwestern landscape the way a hunters' camp gumbo I found in an old Southern cookbook has become part of my version of Louisiana: water, spices, duck gizzards and livers slow simmered in a cast iron kettle—a dark proto-gumbo detectable five miles downwind. In coastal Washington it's salmon marinated in elderberry juice, Salish style. In south Texas I consider the brush-buster half-breed Longhorn men traveling for days with a pouch of cornmeal and a handful of *carne seca*, mixing crushed red chilies into their coffee grounds for the evening pot.

And in north Texas I think of the Joads. Although Route 66, the main artery for many of Steinbeck's immigrants, has been largely superseded, its lesser tributaries through Oklahoma into the Texas panhandle and its kingbird towns still spark memories of the Joads. A kingbird town is a phenomenon endemic to the Great Plains: small dry villages where on summer afternoons the only sound and sign of life is the chatter and squabble of kingbirds in the wind-bent Chinese elms. Rarely, you might hear a rooster crow, or a large blow fly, or a tentative screen-door in the distance. A breeze might pick up a little dust funnel and sweep it across the gas station lot; this ignites a fresh chorus from the excitable kingbirds in the trees along the fence.

These are the sort of towns the Joads clattered through early in their book, worried and continually vulnerable, but creating an invaluable repository of rock-bottom Okie speech ("Pa'd crap a litter of lizards") and eating some of the most desperate, haunting food in literature. Texola. Shamrock. Groom.

Mostly the Joads ate America's first domestic meat and its staple for two centuries, pork. At their frail camps along 66 they ate their home-packed salt-pork while it lasted and ate boiled potatoes—just boiled potatoes—when it was gone. Somewhere along the line they managed a couple of pounds of fresh sidemeat; somewhere they ate nothing but cornmeal mush. Six adults and a pair of children. Somewhere else on a good day, pork chops; a week later nothing but fried dough. Joad food. Food that smells wonderful and can change the color of your eyes and skin.

Driving north through the panhandle from Plains to Perryton last summer I thought about the Joads and the Beaufort scale and the general aeolian on and off all day. I even stopped to take a picture of what I assumed was old 66 paralleling the interstate. One could probably do a lively business selling chunks of that pavement in Japanese Americana shops.

By the time I reached Perryton, high in the panhandle, I had a healthy appetite worked up and knew exactly what I wanted. I sneaked the hotplate into the motel room and drove to a grocery for a pound of hamburger. I had a few red potatoes rolling around in the back seat. I cracked all the motel room windows and set up the hotplate in a corner far from the smoke detector. I made two oblong hamburg steaks and set them to fry over one burner and cut up two potatoes to boil over the other. Nice and easy does it.

I sipped a glass of George Dickel and watched the kingbirds tussle on a telephone wire and wondered at the organizational network and ethnoeconomic currents that brought the East Indian family—one of Indic scores in the hostelry profession throughout the west—to own this particular panhandle motel. I thought of Tom Joad describing something or other as "drier than a bitch monkey."

When the spuds were soft and the meat crispy (I had moved the operation to the luggage stand beside the half-open door and fanned the worst of the grease smoke out with a highway map), I poured off most of the fat and stirred in enough flour and tap-water to make a peppery mudpuddle gravy and spooned it over everything on the plastic plate.

And there it was. With the kingbird racket outside and traces of a mockingbird a block away, the meal dovetailed into the cultural geography tightly enough to feel almost macrobiotic. Eat it fast, sop with big-time white bread, and serve, like all Joad food, with "hot black coffee."

Twenty-Three

From Bear Butte

The tumbleweed arrived in immigrant flax seed, Bon Homme County, South Dakota, in 1873.

Aquatic Life arrives annually in intermittent prairie ponds (those isolated puddles that come and go from season to season and need constant attention) in the form of tiny crustacean eggs and seed shrimp carried on the feet of killdeer.

Cholera—the worst scourge since the plague—arrived on the northern plains in 1833, the far-flung spurt (says DeVoto) of the great Asian epidemic of 1816 that finally spilled forth from India via the Ganges delta in 1826, reached the Caspian by '29 and ravaged Russia in '30, Mecca in '31 (hence spread by terrified pilgrims), across the Black Sea, up the Danube into and over Europe, wasting the British Isles in 1832, the year Irish emigrants introduced it to Canada, where it flowed up the St. Lawrence and down the canals to Albany, down the Hudson to New York, westward via the Ohio and the Erie canal until in '33 the interior Mississippi valley was aflame, sending its last flagging but still devastating finger up the Missouri as far as Fort Union, near the present Montana/North Dakota line.

——————

From the top of Bear Butte—a sacred mountain for several native tribes, site of mythic origins, visitation, primal instruction from the culture heroes—I scan the Black Hills and their peaks named fatuously after men, but my field glasses continually drift back to the dilapidated hulk of the 1938 WPA "beach house" down by Bear Butte Lake, a stone-in-matrix relic somehow pathetic in its brief life and early ruination, an entropic splinter-wince from the tender 1930s.

To the near north, below, that run-off beauty, again, of rivers building. A fleet of junked cars on a green slope two miles off (a wet summer, 1986) form a sort of fancy cattle brand design, a giant inadvertent Lazy J-7. A neat square of segregated white bee hives way out there looks New English, Congregational.

This entire upper butte is aflutter with prayer offerings, as it must have been in 1833 and perhaps 1533 — bright ribbons looped in the trees, yard goods tied in the branches, yellow bandanas, little cotton Bull Durham sacks rocking in the wind with the pine boughs, skeins of red yarn knotted to limbs, strips of ripped shirt. . . . (It all flashes spectacularly off and on as the sun goes in/comes out from scudding cloudlets.) Oh want and crush and cry and yarrow — Does the Doublemint wrapper dropped along the trail count too?

TWENTY-FOUR

This rainy Saturday morning on the Missouri River the wife and I are curled up in the back of the pickup snug and dry, reading snatches of Montaniana in a day-old (as in bread or donuts) Lewistown newspaper.

Someone killed a bear last week in the foothills of the Judith Mountains, 50 miles southwest of here. It was "jet black and big. I thought it was one of those yearling Angus steers when he first came out of the timber."

Elsewhere, a native son of Belt, Montana, a village of 600 head 75 miles on west from the Judiths, was just married in Vienna, Austria. After studying music at the University of Montana, then taking a Masters at Notre Dame, he is currently in advanced opera studies over there. His wife is a recent Sorbonne graduate. *Wien bleibt Wien.*

Outside, the raggy clouds are low over the Missouri. This is one of the last free-flowing, damless sections of the river. Its bluffs and breaks show slag-brown undertones from the wet shale. Dark ponderosas congregate in coulees; sagebrush covers the bottom-land benches, set off by blooming patches of rabbit-brush, the big weed rumored to be capable of producing gasoline. The river glints in clipped glimpses to the east. Cattle bawl from the valley below.

The image of Lewis and Clark moving up this river, one day at a time, as my mother would say, nags and pulls me back for a damp cigarette again and again and in the end disturbs. The Lewis and Clark expedition—one of this continent's top contenders for Homeric saga status; one of the major ceremonial (if we didn't know better) movements of white men on North America; a mission with the spiritual potential inherent in the bestowing of names — now that has, if nothing else at this late date, operatic possibilities. The scale is perfect, some 40 men and a woman, a stagefull, with York as basso profundo and assorted moveable mounted cardboard silhouettes appearing and reappearing on bluish distant bluffs.

Those 40 men and their terra incognita. They were gone three years, as long as Nantucket whalers' terms. Books on the expedition are rampant as those on that other western mytho-morph, George Armstrong Custer. New editions of the Journals appear regularly. There are hundreds of historical markers along the expedition's various routes. There are Lewiston, Idaho, and Clarkston, Washington, facing each other across the Snake. There are countless motels, drive-ins, and auto parts shops bearing the names of the two leaders. There is Lewis's woodpecker and Clark's nutcracker and no doubt they occasionally grace the same high country pine. There is Lewis and Clark gin, out of Helena, and much much more.

In 1952 I read a sizeable chunk of the journals aloud to my father who was bed-ridden with the flu. I remember the handsome makeshift spelling, as if written on wood with a nail; the steady geo-tick of the days and foot-miles; the half-drawn shades in the sick room and the lilacs beyond. But here, or at any of those historical markers across the west, it all disturbs in the end. The microscopic image of those men bobs and is lost in late 20th Century spleen.

With Custer it is different. Over the years there congealed a concrete composite image of that man from the many photographs, an image gathered about his chin. It is a point I can grasp phrenologically. It is a key and a punctum, thanks, I assume, to a child-hood and youth spent in the general's home state, where I was exposed at frequent intervals to similar chins on a similar phiz.

I remember them leaning beside gas station candy machines smoking during the school lunch hour. Or shooting mid-morning games of eight-ball in rural roadhouses, looking up asquint in the shaft of sun-light when the door opened. Or telling stories in the restroom at high school dances about shotgunning cats from cars by night on country roads. Their faces showed up in class pictures only to disappear a year or two later. Some would rematerialize one Saturday morning, back at the gas station, leaning there all day with a butch haircut and new army fatigues.

When I was ten I got to know a boy named Dooley. We would run into each other once in a while catfishing at the lake. We shared a lantern's light a couple of evenings while we fished. His utter devotion to the pastime attracted me. He wore a ducktail hair-cut and possessed a bottomless repertoire of filthy stories and juicy curses. Late at night he composed dirty ditties about some of our teachers. Years later in sophomore health class Dooley was the one who volunteered a fervent straight-faced version of the perennial "Spanish Fly in the 7-Up" story that had the rest of us squirming in our seats. Out in the hollow behind the school, Dooley, using some mysterious fist hold, could urinate a good 12 feet. Shortly after high school Dooley and a pair of his local buddies were arrested while robbing a gun store somewhere in western Indiana. Two of the three had Custer's chin.

Lewis and Clark, though, are so far gone, so two-dimensional and frescoed in the national imagination, that to stand here on the spot thinking of them is, in the end, disturbing. No access, no focus, most of the river a stultified pool for water skiers. Some locked-in January I'll go through the big facsimile edition of the journals looking for punctum.

Just upstream from here, for starters, some 2,000 miles and 379 days out of St. Louis, they first gave a woman's name to a river.

The sky clears by forenoon and we head south. A golden eagle sits on a knoll near the road; it resembles a big black dog on its haunches.

At Grassrange we stop for coffee and find home-made rhubarb-custard pie. By the time we leave the cafe the sun is full out. The Judiths hang dark on the skyline, as some detached emblematic range will from most points in Montana. Over toward the gas station, at the edge of the gravelled parking lot, there's a rummage sale setting up. Racks of used clothing flap below the Conoco sign.

Milling around the long folding tables covered with odds and ends are a dozen Hutterite girls—I mean teenagers and young women—in long checkered skirts, kerchieves and bonnets and snug high-necked

velveteen jackets. Their palette is infinitely brighter
than that of the Amish and Mennonites back east.
Driven, ancestrally, from Moravia and the Tirol, then
from the Ukraine and Hungary for their pacifist
ways, from the U.S. into Canada for World War II,
they flutter here, bright commotion in the new sunlight,
chattering in heavy indecipherable accents, teasing
with squirt guns and third-hand toys. They are fair
and slightly off-set, with a touch of the plain wild.
They wear short workaday fingernails; straw and
palomino tufts of hair show from under their headgear.
One buys a used Eddie Rabbit album; another a
beat-up paperback copy of *The Winds of War*.

TWENTY-FIVE

spread the cheap East Indian sheet atop the east
Pawnee Butte in Weld County, Colorado, and sit in
the mid-morning September sun. I have been craving
heights like a cat. Meadowlark calls and hereford
coughs float up faint and dislocated from far below.
Big cumulus clouds throw their east-bound shadows
on the plains. Through field glasses I spy a badger
shuffling and nosing along one of the arroyo walls in
the fierce Pawnee Creek drainage pattern at the base
of the butte.

Up here, close at hand, flies drone; a Say's
phoebe family suns. Rock wrens, creatures of the
edges, comb the lip of the butte and the nearby escarpment daily, picking and feeding, a troupe of eight at
the moment, there after every shower or blow,
exploring the newly eroded edge, maybe an eighth of
an inch more exposed than yesterday.

I was basking, idly envisioning a conceptual core
sample of the Great Plains poetic magma, a dotted
line connecting the hamlets of Orion, Seven Persons,
and Many Berries, Alberta, the triangle to be cut and
plucked like a melon sample, when, way out there, I
saw a speck of color move. I found it through the
glasses: a hiker, wearing a backpack, cutting across the
grasslands toward the escarpment on a course that
would pass within half a mile of the butte.

Blue t-shirt and cut-off shorts. A girl or young
woman, I think. She rises and falls, crests and
disappears on the topography like a small boat at sea.
Her pace is steady and efficient; her walk unique and
thoughtful; her thumbs seem hooked in her belt in

a contemplative way. At one point she stops and stoops to examine something along the trail, a track or dead bee. A yellow kerchief is tied around her head.

Finally she passes the butte at her nearest tangent and continues south-southwest. As she recedes now, I realize I've been watching her, completely absorbed, for fifteen minutes. And now as she moves away there's something more desperate about the thing. I'm not so far from home, I'm not so long alone, but for a minute there when I'd thought I'd lost her for good over one of the rises it was small-scale panic. Then, a minute later, she surfaced again, moving steadily. After another ten minutes all I could pick up was the occasional flash of the backs of her alternating calves in the sunlight. I never did see exactly where she entered or climbed the escarpment. For the next hour as I descended the butte and hiked off myself in the same general direction I half expected to see her topping a ridge in the distance and kept a nonchalant eye out for a footprint.

It is part of the valence of the plains, part of the endless looking, the hard squint. It is the space in the face you see in certain of Edward Curtis's portraits of prairie people. Watching any human figure in this setting for half an hour stirs the tendency to form a bond; or even, some days, in a vague aerated way, to fall in love.

Yesterday at daybreak I was up and sipping coffee in the chilly air. From the Crow Creek campground

trees came a steady chorus of small sounds from
early fall migrants in the only real grove for many
miles. The coyotes had been in top form all night
and continued sporadically after sun-up, alternating
with the roosters of Briggsdale a mile away. After a
century of reciprocal influence the two sounds are
curiously similar.

The morning was so clear as I drove out to the
creek that things were magnified, slightly oversized—
a marsh hawk loomed as it quartered the short-grass
prairie and the Rockies shone loud on the horizon.

I parked and headed off up the creek. The
summer had been a dry one and most of the holes
that usually held water—modest quarter-moon wet
spots from 10 to 40 feet long, just enough for teal—
were dry. Rabbitbrush and snakeweed bloom
brightened the blanched buffalo/grama grass rolling
away. A handful of yucca showed dark on a far rise.
Here and there a horned toad scurried.

There's a paleolithic feel to this solo plains teal
shooting that has always engaged me: the long hikes
across the plains, the slow crouch and crawl on the
hands and knees through the prickly pear to get within
range. If you miss or spook the ducks at one spot,
the next one might be a mile farther on; by mid-day
you're so far away from everything you break into
a commemorative fandango.

Finally, an hour from the car, I found a fair-sized
puddle of water. As I edged in I saw ripples emanat-
ing from the near bank and knew there were ducks.
Seconds later four blue-wings jumped and I shot two.

One dropped in the water, so I retrieved the bird from the grass and sat down to clean it while the breeze slowly nudged the other one in towards shore. Somewhere off in the Pawnee grasslands, down one of those ingratiating two-rut dirt roads that lead to blasted shells of ranches abandoned in dust-bowl terror, someone was sighting in a rifle—*p-pow, p-pow, p-pow.* . . .

Late afternoon I split the birds, rub them down with butter and salt and pepper and grill them over a half-wood/half-charcoal fire with sweet potatoes banked along the edges. Deep meat, dark and Orphean as liver, washed down with a bargain burgundy before the mosquitos get too bad.

After dinner I walk over to the old half-wild ball diamond on the north edge of the grounds. There's no one else in the area. Sunflowers grow along the baselines and here and there across the outfield. A thick row of them crowds close around the backstop fence.

It is all bathed by the peculiar pearly, second-magnitude glow of early twilight. Utter silence. The white metal posts of the outfield fence trace a gentle digital arc, a geometry brilliant and beneficent as a gift. The Chinese elms on the low ridge beyond sink from green to umber. The tall wooden light poles emerge as delicate, filled with the momentary peace of *things done*, lovely with the afterlight reflecting from their common western edges. It is a culture. It is a people, now, in this place; an arrangement of things in space. As on the legends of maps from the wilder arctic, where *culture* connotes a simple toehold, a passable road or jeep path.

What's left on the plains that speak of the plains, from the plains, with the deep chords and roundness of things long-in-place and timeless in intent? Coyote, good friend and great Digester. Some of the most telling highway stretches in the world. Cattlemen in winter. Faces at Standing Rock. The way today's Comanche settlements in Oklahoma reflect in minia-ture the territorial layout of the tribal bands in the nomadic days. The sky and the longspurs and the fugi-tive native grasses and thousands of mouths to feed. Up in Wyoming, a man named Geno Dreamer.

What's gone, gone forever? Most of the kit foxes. The Mandans' buckskin Map of the World and the field songs of their women. Most of the prairie chickens. Who knows how many tongues, entire mind/heart/body systems, languages that eddied onto the plains to be lost forever—just gone, people unheard of again, like the mysterious A's, or simply squashed one afternoon, like the Ku'ato, a Kiowa band with a distinct dialect exterminated about 1770 by the Sioux "somewhere near the Black Hills." (The thought of the extinguished songs and soft words is the hardest.) Most of the elk-eye aphrodisiacs.

There is still the space so powerful as to render time silly. And the land continually challenging, calling for the worthy words: *quaver* and *rip*, *ekto* and *endo*. There are the mobile mixed-blood garlic-loving peoples plains-destined somewhere in the future; they will thrive by virtue of their sense of skyline.

And there is the crusty artifact I brought in this morning with the teal: a fence weight, I think—a shoe-box sized chunk of beige stone I found in the midst of nowhere out there, bound neatly a generation or two back with heavy wire, once around each way and knotted, Christmas present fashion. Cut and tied and used well enough to admire for a day on the campground table. Maybe I'll take it home to the wife tomorrow. Maybe I'll leave it on the pitcher's mound. It is an eloquent, cultured thing.

The Poetics of Space, Gaston Bachelard (translated by Maria Jolas). Beacon Press, 1969.

The Idea of Landscape and the Sense of Place, John Barrell. Cambridge University, 1972.

When Stars Came Down to Earth, Von Del Chamberlain. Ballena Press, 1982.

The Prairie World, David Costello. Crowell, 1969.

Across the Wide Missouri, Bernard DeVoto. Houghton-Mifflin, 1947.

The Blackfeet, John C. Ewers. University of Oklahoma, 1958.

The Fighting Cheyennes, George B. Grinnell. Scribner, 1915.

The Life of George Bent, ed. by George Hyde. University of Oklahoma, 1968.

Birds of the Great Plains, Paul Johngard. University of Nebraska, 1979.

The Great Plains in Transition, C. F. Kraenzel. University of Oklahoma, 1955.

The Arapaho, Alfred L. Kroeber. American Museum of Natural History, 1907.

The Peyote Cult, Weston La Barre. Schocken Books, 1969.

The Grassland of North America: Prolegomena to Its History, James C. Malin, P. Smith, 1967.

The Kiowas, Mildred Mayhall. University of Oklahoma, 1962.

The American Language, H. L. Mencken. Abridged edition, Knopf, 1963.

The Village Indians of the Upper Missouri, Roy W. Meyer. University of Nebraska, 1977.

The Indian and the Horse, Frank G. Roe. University of Oklahoma, 1955.

Lakota Names and Traditional Uses of Native Plants by Sicangu (Brule) People in the Rosebud Area, S.D., Dilwyn Rogers. The Rosebud Educational Society, 1980.

The Arapahoes — Our People, Virginia C. Trenholm. University of Oklahoma, 1970.

The Great Plains, Walter P. Webb. Ginn and Co., 1931.

Prehistoric Man on the Great Plains, Waldo Wedel. University of Oklahoma, 1961.

Corn Among the Indians of the Upper Missouri, George F. Will and George Hyde. University of Nebraska, 1964.

ABOUT THE AUTHOR

Merrill Gilfillan was born in Ohio and now
lives in the upper White River country
of northwest Nebraska. He is the author of
several books of poetry and is currently
completing a volume of short stories from the
northern plains.

DATE DUE

5 June 93			
MAY 0 4 1995			